booksonline

Read this book online today:

With SAP PRESS BooksOnline we offer you online access to knowledge from
the leading SAP experts. Whether you use it as a beneficial supplement or as
an alternative to the printed book, with SAP PRESS BooksOnline you can:

• Access your book anywhere, at any time. All you need is an Internet connection.
• Perform full text searches on your book and on the entire SAP PRESS library.
• Build your own personalized SAP library.

The SAP PRESS customer advantage:

Register this book today at *www.sap-press.com* and obtain exclusive free trial
access to its online version. If you like it (and we think you will), you can choose to
purchase permanent, unrestricted access to the online edition at a very special price!

Here's how to get started:

1. Visit *www.sap-press.com*.
2. Click on the link for SAP PRESS BooksOnline and login (or create an account).
3. Enter your free trial license key, shown below in the corner of the page.
4. Try out your online book with full, unrestricted access for a limited time!

Your personal free trial **license key**
for this online book is:
bvgt-7c9m-e5xp-faid

ABAP™ Development for Materials Management in SAP®:
User Exits and BAdIs

 PRESS

SAP® Essentials

Expert SAP knowledge for your day-to-day work

Whether you wish to expand your SAP knowledge, deepen it, or master a use case, SAP Essentials provide you with targeted expert knowledge that helps support you in your day-to-day work. To the point, detailed, and ready to use.

SAP PRESS is a joint initiative of SAP and Galileo Press. The know-how offered by SAP specialists combined with the expertise of the Galileo Press publishing house offers the reader expert books in the field. SAP PRESS features first-hand information and expert advice, and provides useful skills for professional decision-making.

SAP PRESS offers a variety of books on technical and business related topics for the SAP user. For further information, please visit our website: *www.sap-press.com.*

Martina Kaplan, Christian Oehler
Implementing SAP Enhancement Packages
2010, app. 220 pp.
978-1-59229-351-3

Michael Englbrecht, Michael Wegelin
SAP Interface Programming
2009, app. 405 pp.
978-1-59229-318-6

Harald Röser
SAP Controls Workshop: SAP PRESS Essentials 10
2005, app. 165 pp.
978-1-59229-073-4

Horst Keller
The Official ABAP Reference
2nd ed. 2005, app. 1,213 pp.
978-1-59229-039-0

Jürgen Schwaninger

ABAP™ Development for Materials Management in SAP®: User Exits and BAdIs

Galileo Press

Bonn • Boston

Galileo Press is named after the Italian physicist, mathematician and philosopher Galileo Galilei (1564–1642). He is known as one of the founders of modern science and an advocate of our contemporary, heliocentric worldview. His words *Eppur si muove* (And yet it moves) have become legendary. The Galileo Press logo depicts Jupiter orbited by the four Galilean moons, which were discovered by Galileo in 1610.

Editor Stefan Proksch
English Edition Editor Laura Korslund
Translation Lemoine International, Inc., Salt Lake City, UT
Copyeditor Julie McNamee
Cover Design Graham Geary
Photo Credit iStockphoto/ValentynVolkov
Layout Design Vera Brauner
Production Manager Kelly O'Callaghan
Assistant Production Editor Graham Geary
Typesetting Publishers' Design and Production Services, Inc.
Printed and bound in Canada

ISBN 978-1-59229-373-5

© 2011 by Galileo Press Inc., Boston (MA)

1st Edition 2011

1st German edition published 2010 by Galileo Press, Bonn, Germany

Library of Congress Cataloging-in-Publication Data
Schwaninger, Jürgen.
  [ABAP-Programmierung für die SAP-Materialwirtschaft. English]
  ABAP development for materials management in SAP : user exits and BAdis /
Jürgen Schwaninger. — 1st ed.
      p. cm.
  Includes index.
  ISBN-13: 978-1-59229-373-5
  ISBN-10: 1-59229-373-5
  1. Materials management—Computer programs. 2. SAP ERP. 3. Object-oriented programming
(Computer science) I. Title.
  TS161.S38713 2011
  658.70285'536—dc22
2010042024

Contents at a Glance

Dear Reader,

Since the days of R/3, programmers have had the option to enhance and optimize the SAP standard with individual and unique ABAP programs. However, it is no longer enough to have the skills to implement a requirement in ABAP, especially in a comprehensive functionality such as Materials Management in SAP ERP. Programmers must take their education further by understanding how and where to find the correct user exit for each project.

In his daily work, Jürgen Schwaninger is an SAP consultant and deals with the most frequently made customer queries regarding user exits. Based on his amount of experience, he knows the tried-and-tested solutions for these complex problems, and has carefully selected the most helpful and concise examples from his repertoire, which you can directly apply to your daily work. Not only does this book provide helpful real-life tutorials, which show you the precise procedures and the respective codings to achieve a solution, along with possible alternatives, this book also provides you with systematic access to all user exits, BAdIs, and enhancement spots in MM.

We welcome you to share any praise or critical comments that will help us improve our books. Our number one goal is to provide accurate and useful information to benefit you, the reader, and to improve and expand your skills. We encourage you to visit our website at *www.sap-press.com* and share your feedback about this work.

Thank you for purchasing a book from SAP PRESS!

Laura Korslund
Editor, SAP PRESS

Galileo Press
100 Grossman Drive, Suite 205
Braintree, MA 02184

Laura.Korslund@galileo-press.com
www.sap-press.com

Contents

Preface

Some things happen in a surprising way. Just like when the editor from SAP PRESS asked whether I'd be interested in writing a book on user exits and BAdIs in Materials Management (MM). At that time, I had already started writing a small online book on ABAP Debugger, but writing a proper book was something completely different. However, over the many years of working as a logistics consultant and developer, I have probably programmed hundreds of enhancements for customers, so I thought, why not?

More difficult than making this decision was deciding how the book should be structured. From the start, it was clear that covering all enhancement options in detail was impossible because there are so many options in SAP Materials Management (which we will refer to in this book primarily as MM). On the other hand, I didn't want to create an incomplete overview of the available enhancements; there are enough gaps already in the official documentation. To meet this challenge, this book describes individually selected enhancements in detail in the main chapters, with priority given particularly to the more complex and difficult enhancements. All other user exits and BAdIs are given a structured and complete overview in the Appendix.

Now that the book is complete, I would like to thank all those who helped me implement this project. Kristina Noe and Philipp Grimm are especially mentioned here. I would also like to thank Stefan Proksch from the SAP PRESS editorial office in Germany very much for his tremendous help.

A special thank you goes to my family who gave me the necessary time on short weekends to write this book.

Jürgen Schwaninger
Senior Logistics & ABAP Consultant

1   Introduction

The Materials Management functionality in SAP ERP, which in this book we'll refer to as Materials Management, or MM, is certainly among the largest of its type. The settings in Customizing are therefore especially comprehensive. The customer processes are also extremely complex and multivariant in this area so that the limits of customizing are reached sooner or later.

1.1   Objectives

To cope with the required processes, SAP provides a large number of user exits and BAdIs in MM that allow you to implement highly individual requirements and processes. This book shows you the options available and describes the exact procedure for selecting enhancements so that you can use this technology to optimize your processes.

First of all, you will learn how to generally deal with enhancements, BAdIs, and enhancement spots so that you can easily understand the examples given in this book. The use and programming of selected enhancements in ABAP are described using step-by-step instructions. All ABAP listings are fully displayed with detailed comments so that you can easily apply them in your own custom applications.

1.2   Structure and Content

If you don't program enhancements very often, you can familiarize yourself with the concepts of user exits, BAdIs, and enhancement spots in **Chapter 2**. The use and activation of these enhancement options are described based on brief examples.

Chapters follow for each of the major areas in MM: Purchasing (**Chapter 3**), External Services Management (**Chapter 4**), Inventory Management (**Chapter 5**), Evaluation and Account Assignment Area (**Chapter 6**), and Logistics Invoice Verification (**Chapter 7**). The most important and most comprehensive enhancement options are described using simple examples to avoid any unnecessary confusion.

Because problems are rarely identical, examples are used that convey fundamental functions and options. With this knowledge, you can transfer your individual requirement to the enhancement.

The book concludes with a brief look at the validation and substitution of accounting documents in **Chapter 8**. With regard to posting goods movements and incoming invoices in MM, accounting documents are also automatically generated as follow-on documents in SAP ERP Financials Financial Accounting, which we'll refer to as Financial Accounting, or FI. Users frequently want to add additional data from MM to this FI document or use additional checks from the accounting point of view. This technology can also be used as a replacement for possible available custom checks in user units or BAdIs because you can build up a central set of rules in one place, regardless of whether a document comes from the Inventory Management, the Logistics Invoice Verification, or the FI system itself.

Appendix A provides an overview of the user exits and BAdIs in in MM. The Appendix is divided into the same areas as the chapters of this book. Areas that have many enhancements are further structured so that you can quickly find all available enhancements on a specific transaction or on a specific procedure.

1.3 Target Audience

This book is mainly aimed at MM consultants who only have a basic knowledge of ABAP, but it's also for experienced ABAP programmers who may have little knowledge of MM. However, even if you are an experienced MM consultant and programmer, you can use this book as a reference guide and perhaps even learn one or two tricks.

Whichever group you belong to, rest assured that this book offers the necessary coverage of ABAP and logistics without straying far from the fundamentals.

1.4 Prerequisites

Although this book is primarily aimed at consultants with little experience in programming, you should have the fundamental ABAP knowledge at the SAP BC400 training level. The use of ABAP objects, unless absolutely necessary, has been omitted. Nevertheless, there are individual BAdIs that have an object-oriented approach, which must be kept in the programming.

However, you don't need any deep knowledge in object-oriented programming. Knowledge of the essential basic concepts of object orientation is enough in these cases. Some special features of object orientation in this book, such as interfaces or upcast implementations, are only described briefly.

The examples can in principle be understood in each R/3 system from Release 4.6C, or in an SAP ERP Central Component system from Release 5.0. Some enhancements have only been introduced in a later release and are therefore only available in more recent SAP systems. Appendix A provides the prerequisites for specific enhancements.

2 General Information on User Exits and BAdIs

You've possibly purchased this book because you already have a good understanding of SAP components for Materials Management (MM), but you only have a fundamental knowledge of ABAP programming. Perhaps you program more frequently but have little contact with the latest technologies, such as the enhancement spots that will gradually replace the classic BAdIs.

User exits, BAdIs, and enhancement spots fulfill the same purpose. When SAP applications and programs run according to a predefined schema that doesn't always precisely fit in with your enterprise requirements, a navigation option is provided with enhancements in positions selected by SAP, which you can use to exit the standard coding. You can activate these navigation options, if necessary, and assign your own ABAP code, which means you can change data provided in a defined interface or completely integrate your custom functions here.

In this chapter, the various enhancement options are introduced and explained using a step-by-step example. If you've already implemented numerous enhancements in SAP systems, and you're only searching for specific information on MM, feel free to skip this chapter.

2.1 Using User Exits

User exits constitute the oldest SAP enhancement technology still in use today. In this section, the main focus is on dealing fundamentally with user exits. To better illustrate the technology, the following example shows how you can use and activate user exits: If a purchase requisition is converted into an order, this is logged in the change documents of the purchase requisition using enhancement `MM06E007`.

> **Concepts from the World of User Exits**
>
> Numerous concepts are important for understanding user exits:
>
> ▶ **Enhancement**
> Enhancements are provided by SAP and include one or several components that, as a whole, allow for a defined functionality.
>
> ▶ **Components**
> Components are the elements of an enhancement that are ultimately used to customize the standard. Components can be exit modules or dynpros for custom-specific fields.
>
> ▶ **Projects**
> Projects are created by the customer to include enhancements (and components). Projects can be activated and deactivated at any time. However, only components from active projects can be actually carried out.

2.1.1 Finding and Viewing Enhancements

Finding the suitable enhancement for a planned project can be difficult. Lists of enhancements are usually available in the SAP Implementation Guide (SAP REFERENCE IMG in CUSTOMIZING, Transaction SPRO). However, the Repository Info System that you can find via Transaction SMOD in the UTILITIES • FIND menu can also be a good starting point. You now also have this book for MM, and with it a virtually complete overview on all the enhancements available (see Appendix A).

If you've found a promising enhancement, you can also view this in Transaction SMOD. Besides the documentation, you can also take a brief look at the components included here.

2.1.2 Creating a Project and Assigning Enhancements

To use the previously mentioned MM06E007 enhancement, you must first create a project.

You can implement this via Transaction CMOD or via the TOOLS • ABAP WORKBENCH • UTILITIES • ENHANCEMENTS • PROJECT MANAGEMENT menu path.

1. Choose a project name in this dialog box, for example, ZMM06E07 (see Figure 2.1), and then click CREATE.

Figure 2.1 Creating a Project

2. Enter a short text describing the project, and then click ENHANCEMENT ASSIGN-MENT. Confirm the subsequent query and whether the project should be saved.

3. Assign the `MM06E007` enhancement to the project in the next screen (see Figure 2.2). Save the project again.

Figure 2.2 Adding an Enhancement

2.1.3   Using Components of the Project

After you've successfully created your project, you can use one component and integrate custom ABAP code:

1. Display the project again in Transaction CMOD, and then click the COMPO-NENTS button.

2. You can now only see one component here: `EXIT_SAPMM06E_020`. Double-click this component to directly go to the Function Builder (Transaction SE37). Your custom coding isn't directly stored in the function module, however, because it's in the SAP name range. In fact, each exit automatically includes an include statement for a Z include. In the example given, this is the `ZXM06U50` include.

3. Double-click `ZXM06U50` in the source text. You receive a brief note indicating that includes, the names of which begin with "ZX...," are reserved for user exits. Because you are creating this kind of include, confirm the note via the `Enter` key. When asked if the include should be created, choose YES.

4. Copy the coding from Listing 2.1, and activate the include. Be sure to customize the queried company code to your existing test data.

```
*&---------------------------------------------------------------------*
*&  Include           ZXM06U50
*&---------------------------------------------------------------------*
* Generate change
document in purchase requisition, if it is converted into
* a follow-on document. The parameter c_changedoc_for_req
* must be defined for this.

* i_ekko-bstyp " Only if the follow-on document is a purchase order
* i_ekko-bukrs " Only for company code 1000
IF     i_ekko-bstyp = 'F'
   AND i_ekko-bukrs = '1000'.

* Generate change document
  c_changedoc_for_req = 'X'.
ENDIF.
```

Listing 2.1 Example — Generating a Change Document

The user exit is checked to determine whether the follow-up document is a purchase order (field `i_ekko-bstyp` = 'F') and whether the procedure is carried out in company code 1000 (field `i_ekko-bukrs`). In this case, a change document is generated. The field `c_changedoc_for_req` is therefore defined.

> **Note**
>
> After you've created the include, you can see a green checkmark in the overview of the components (see Figure 2.3). This indicates that the Z include exists but not that coding exists in it.
>
> Furthermore, you can always see a red dot next to the PROJECT text in this view. This indicates that your project isn't yet active. Your coding is therefore not implemented.

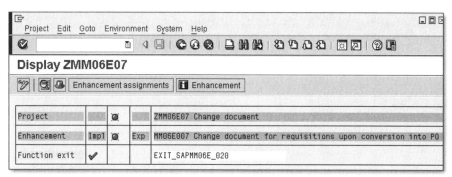

Figure 2.3 Overview of Components

2.1.4   Activating and Deactivating Projects

You must now activate the project so that the user exit is actually implemented. You can do this directly in the initial screen of Transaction CMOD (see Figure 2.4).

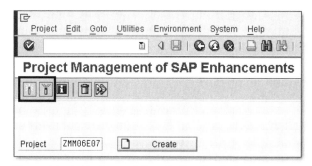

Figure 2.4 Activating and Deactivating the Projects

1. Choose PROJECT • ACTIVATE PROJECT in the menu, or click the respective icon in the initial view.

2. If the system doesn't behave as expected, it may be sensible to deactivate the project to maintain the standard behavior again. To do this, choose PROJECT • DEACTIVATE PROJECT in the menu or click the respective icon.

Several Enhancements in the Project?

Although you can assign several enhancements, you can only activate or deactivate projects as a unit. Only merge the enhancements if they also functionally belong together in their implementation; that is, they implement a specific process.

2.2 Use of Classic BAdIs

Business Add-Ins (BAdIs) display the object-oriented variant of the user exits. BAdIs were introduced with Basis Release 4.6D. The first enhancements are therefore available in R/3 Release 4.6B. However, many BAdIs in MM have only been introduced with SAP R/3 Enterprise 4.7.

The example ME_HOLD_PO BAdI shows you how to use this technology. As you probably know, the HOLD function allows you to temporarily save an incomplete purchase order so that this can be further processed at a later stage. This BAdI allows you to prohibit the HOLD function when you create orders, if necessary.

With Release 6.0, the BAdI technology has been updated and integrated into the enhancement framework (see Section 2.3, Use of New BAdIs [Enhancement Spots]). Already existing BAdIs, now referred to as classic BAdIs, haven't been automatically migrated. Both worlds currently exist in parallel.

2.2.1 Finding and Viewing Enhancements

There are also overviews for BAdIs in the SAP IMG (SAP Reference IMG in Customizing, Transaction SPRO). Alternatively, you can find a complete overview of all BAdIs in Appendix A of this book.

You can display the definition of the BAdI via Transaction SE18. Since Basis Release SAP ECC 6.0, you have the choice between searching for ENHANCEMENT SPOTS and BADI NAME. Use the latter field to display the BAdI.

Concepts from the World of BAdIs

With BAdIs, you must differentiate between their definition and implementation:

▸ **Definition**
The definition of a BAdI is fundamentally only a blueprint that describes the BAdI with all of the methods included. The definition doesn't include any executable program parts. You can find the definition of a BAdI in Transaction SE18.

▸ **Implementation**
The implementation of a BAdI is necessary to use the definition. The implementation therefore assumes the properties of the definition and consequently uses the blueprint. You can find the implementation of a BAdI in Transaction SE19.

You can see two switches in the initial screen of the BAdI definition (see Figure 2.5).

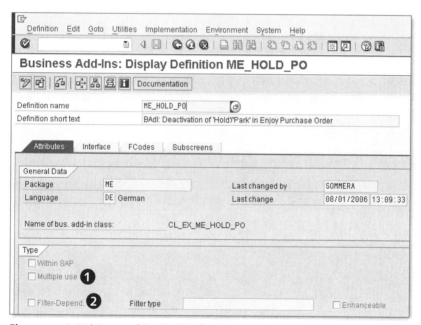

Figure 2.5 Initial Screen of the BAdI Definition

❶ MULTIPLE USE

BAdIs with this switch can be implemented multiple times. All implementations will run directly after one another. However, the sequence cannot be predicted. If you use several processes that use the same BAdI, you can clearly separate these. You can also deactivate an individual implementation without influencing the other processes.

❷ FILTER-DEPEND

Some BAdIs use a filter that you must fill with values when the BAdI is implemented. Typical filter values are, for example, a document type or a country. The BAdI is only started when the filter value transferred during runtime corresponds with the value in your implementation.

In the INTERFACE tab, you can see a list of the methods defined in the BAdI. These methods for the runtime are ultimately called at positions in the program defined by SAP.

1. Double-click the method name to navigate to the class interface, where you can view the input and output parameters of the method.

2. Navigate again to the BAdI via BACK (F3).

3. Click the DOCUMENTATION button in the application bar to see a description of the BAdI.

Numerous BAdIs also contain a sample coding that you can view by choosing the GOTO • SAMPLE CODE • DISPLAY menu path, and then double-clicking a method. You can use this coding as a template for custom enhancements.

2.2.2 Creating a BAdI Implementation

After you've learned the details about the BAdI, you can create an implementation.

1. Start Transaction SE19.

2. The initial screen and the steps to create an implementation differ depending on the Basis release.

   ▶ In a release prior to 7.0, you call your implementation, for example, Z_ME_ HOLD_PO, and click CREATE. In the dialog window that appears, you must now specify the BAdI definition, that is, ME_HOLD_PO, and confirm the entry via Enter .

   ▶ In a release greater or equal to Release 7.0, you choose the CLASSIC BADI option in CREATE IMPLEMENTATION at the bottom of the screen, specify the definition ME_HOLD_PO, and click CREATE IMPLEMENTATION (see Figure 2.6). In the dialog window that appears, enter the name of the implementation, for example, Z_ME_HOLD_PO, and confirm this entry via the Enter key.

Apart from this, there are no release differences worth mentioning with regard to the implementation of BAdIs.

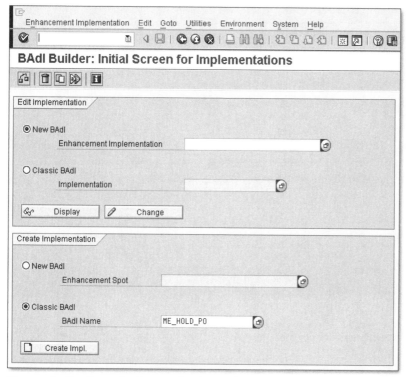

Figure 2.6 Creating an Implementation from Release 7.0

3. Enter a short text as a description of the intended function, and save the BAdI.

2.2.3 Working with Methods

You've now fundamentally prepared the BAdI implementation and can focus on the contained methods.

1. Go to the INTERFACE tab. You can now see the name of classes automatically created and implemented (in the example given, ZCL_IM__ME_HOLD_PO), as well as a list of the methods contained (see Figure 2.7).

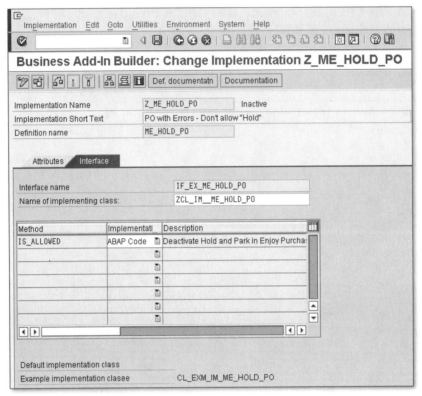

Figure 2.7 Interface of the BAdI Implementation

2. To fill a method with coding, you need to navigate to the list, and double-click the method name IS_ALLOWED.

3. In the method, show the parameter interface by clicking SIGNATURE in the application bar (see Figure 2.8).

   In the example already given, the holding of the order is now prohibited for document type NB (normal purchase order) as long as the document header is still missing. The method obtains, among other things, the import parameter IM_EKKO, which includes the document type in the field BSART, as well as a special flag IM_HEADER_WITH_ERROR, which is set when the document header still contains errors (i.e., a red traffic light icon is displayed in Transaction ME21N). Implement the coding from Listing 2.2.

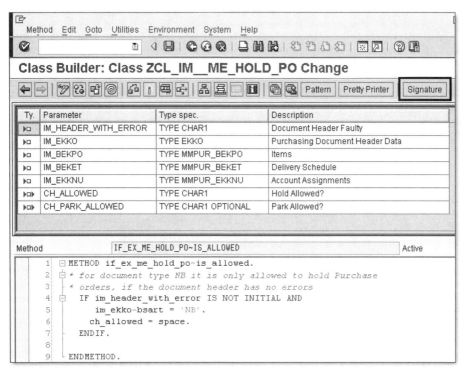

Figure 2.8 Method with Displayed Signature

```
METHOD if_ex_me_hold_po~is_allowed.
*  Purchase orders may only be held for document type NB,
*  if the document header doesn't contain any errors.
    IF im_header_with_error IS NOT INITIAL AND
        im_ekko-bsart = 'NB'.
      ch_allowed = space.
    ENDIF.
ENDMETHOD.
```

Listing 2.2 Example — Prohibiting Holding

4. Save and activate the method, and navigate to the INTERFACE tab of the BAdI via BACK (F3).

2.2.4   Activating and Deactivating BAdIs

You must now activate the enhancement as before with the user exits in the initial screen of the BAdI, so that the BAdI is actually implemented.

1. Ensure that you're in the change mode of the BAdI. You can now activate the BAdI via the menu IMPLEMENTATION • ACTIVATE or the respective icon in the application bar.

2. Create an order with document type NB (Transaction ME21N). The HOLD button is hidden as long as the purchase order header is incomplete.

3. If you want to recover the standard behavior of the purchase order transaction, you can deactivate the BAdI again at any time via the menu IMPLEMENTATION • DEACTIVATE.

2.2.5   Enhanced Editing Options

For more complex BAdIs, you might need to create custom attributes or custom types to have data available that applies to all methods. You can obtain more details on how to use custom attributes in the examples given in Section 3.1, Customized Fields in Purchase Orders, (ME_GUI_PO_CUST), in Chapter 3, and in Section 5.1, Custom Fields in Transaction MIGO, (MB_MIGO_BADI), in Chapter 5.

1. For this, navigate once again to the INTERFACE tab of the BAdI (see Figure 2.9). From this position, navigate by double-clicking the name of the implementing class in the Class Builder.

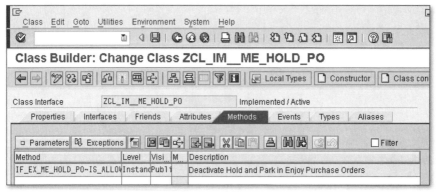

Figure 2.9   Implementing Class in the Class Builder

2. In the TYPES tab, you can define custom data types to use within the class.

3. In the ATTRIBUTES tab, you can create your own variables. As is normally the case in classes, you can also specify the visibility as PRIVATE/PROTECTED or PUBLIC.

You can fundamentally choose PRIVATE here because you'll always remain within the class in the BAdI programming.

4. In the METHODS tab, you can also go to the individual methods to view or change the coding.

2.3 Use of New BAdIs (Enhancement Spots)

With Release 7.0, the BAdIs have been included in SAP Enhancement Framework. However, existing (classic) BAdIs haven't automatically been migrated, but still have the same status.

2.3.1 SAP Enhancement Framework

SAP Enhancement Framework will replace all customization options that exist to date in the long term; that is, user exits and BAdIs, as well as modifications. Using enhancement spots, which identify specific positions of a program or an interface, you can then integrate enhancements at these positions. A distinction is made here between explicit and implicit enhancement spots:

▶ **Explicit enhancement spots**
Explicit enhancement spots are positions defined by a developer in advance where enhancements are possible. These are also partly the new BAdIs, which are integrated as enhancement points. One or several enhancement points are combined into enhancement spots, which you can view in Transaction SE18.

▶ **Implicit enhancement spots**
Implicit enhancement spots are positions in programs that can always be enhanced. Such a position can be found, for example, behind the last line of a program or include, or before the first and behind the last line of the implementation of a procedure. No additional enhancement spot exists for implicit enhancement spots.

Enhancement or Modification?

Implicit enhancement spots are automatically available in all programs and their respective routines. In numerous cases, they are ideal options to customize an SAP program if necessary. Nevertheless, the use of such an enhancement spot is officially still a modification! Only explicit enhancement spots in the form of BAdIs can be used for the "official" enhancement of SAP programs.

2.3.2   Finding and Viewing Enhancement Spots

Just like in the case of user exits and classic BAdIs, you can find enhancement spots in SAP IMG (SAP Reference IMG in Customizing, Transaction SPRO) for MM or in Appendix A of this book.

A brief example for the new BAdIs is also presented to introduce this technology and its respective application. The example uses the ME_POHIST_DISP_CUST BAdI, which can be found in the ES_BADI_ME_POHIST enhancement spot. The display of the purchase order history can be customized using this enhancement.

> **Note**
>
> This section only discusses the differences in classic BAdIs. If you haven't had any experience with classic BAdIs so far, you should first read Section 2.2, Use of Classic BAdIs.

1. You can again display the enhancement spots in Transaction SE18. Enter the name of the enhancement spot and click DISPLAY.

2. You can see the BAdIs contained in the enhancement spot on the left-hand side. Click the ME_POHIST_DISP_CUST BAdI to switch the view to this BAdI (see Figure 2.10).

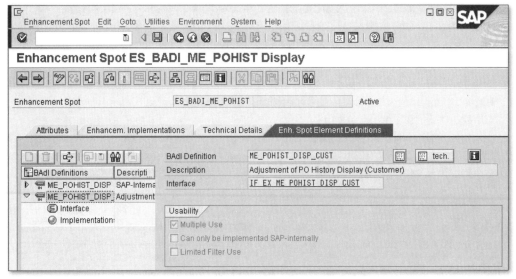

Figure 2.10 Displaying an Enhancement Spot with Contained BAdIs

3. You can then display the documentation for this BAdI via the non-labeled icon on the right-hand side from the name of the BAdI definition.

4. You can view the available methods by double-clicking the name of the interface on the right-hand side (IF_EX_ME_POHIST_DISP_CUST) or by expanding the definition on the left-hand side and then double-clicking INTERFACE.

   To view the parameters, double-click the method, and then click the PARAMETERS button.

2.3.3 Creating Enhancement Implementations

You also create an enhancement implementation in Transaction SE19.

1. Choose the NEW BADI option in the CREATE IMPLEMENTATION area. Enter the name of the enhancement spot, that is, ES_BADI_ME_POHIST, and click CREATE IMPLEMENTATION.

2. In the dialog window that appears (see Figure 2.11), you must specify a name for the enhancement implementation, for example, Z_BADI_ME_POHIST. Enter a short text as a description for this enhancement. You can leave the COMPOSITE ENHANCEMENT IMPLEMENTATION field empty (see the following box). Confirm the dialog to create the enhancement implementation.

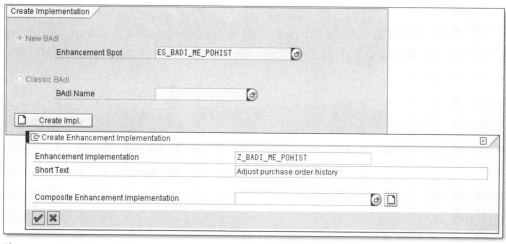

Figure 2.11 Creating an Enhancement Implementation

Composite Enhancement Implementations

You can optionally assign one or several simple enhancement implementations of a composite enhancement implementation. The advantage of this is that several enhancements, which may jointly map a process, are also logically combined in the system. You subsequently have a better overview of the relationships between individual enhancements.

To use a composite enhancement implementation, you enter a name from the customer namespace for the composite enhancement implementation when you create an enhancement implementation (see Figure 2.11). If there still isn't any composite implementation, you can create this directly from this dialog via the icon on the right-hand side of the field.

3. In the dialog window that appears, you can select the implementing BAdIs. Because no input help ($\boxed{\text{F4}}$) is provided here, you can simply close the window via CANCEL ($\boxed{\text{F12}}$).

4. You can select the BAdIs a lot more conveniently in the next dynpro (see Figure 2.12). Here you can see a list of the BAdI implementations on the left-hand side, which is currently still empty. Click the CREATE BAdI IMPLEMENTATION icon, which can be found directly above this area. The dialog window then appears, as shown in Figure 2.12.

5. In this window, you can select the BAdI definition via the input help. Select ME_POHIST_DISP_CUST here. To implement the BAdI, you must still enter the name for the implementation (e.g., ZME_POHIST_DISP_CUST) and for the implementing class (e.g., ZCL_POHIST_DISP_CUST). Enter a short text, and confirm the window by clicking the green checkmark.

6. Confirm the next question on whether the include is supposed to be created by choosing YES.

7. Click ACTIVATE ($\boxed{\text{Ctrl}}$ + $\boxed{\text{F3}}$), and call the implementation and the class generated in the background. This still has nothing to do with the activation of the BAdI (see Section 2.3.5, Activating and Deactivating BAdIs).

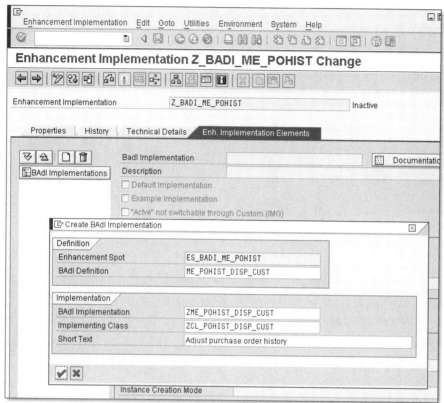

Figure 2.12 Creating a BAdI Implementation

2.3.4 Working with Methods

This path so far has been significantly more time-consuming than with classic BAdIs. However, we can now focus again on the methods and the actual function of the BAdIs.

1. Expand the BAdI implementation on the left-hand side. Double-click the IMPLE-MENTING CLASS entry that appears. The list of the existing methods in the BAdI now appears on the right-hand side (see Figure 2.13).

2. To directly edit a method, double-click the method. You can double-click the implementing class to use the enhanced options of the class. The use of methods is identical to the classic BAdIs, so no further explanation is given here.

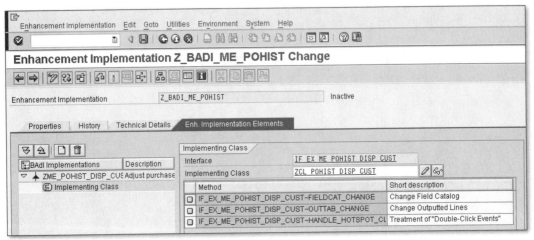

Figure 2.13 Overview of Methods

3. Insert the coding from Listing 2.3 into the method `FIELDCAT_CHANGE`, save, and activate the method. The currency fields are hidden by this coding in the PUR-CHASE ORDER HISTORY tab on the item level of the purchase order so that the user isn't able to see any amounts.

```
METHOD if_ex_me_pohist_disp_cust~fieldcat_change.
* Hide amount and currency key
   DELETE ct_fieldcat WHERE fieldname = 'DMBTR' OR
                            fieldname = 'HSWAE' OR
                            fieldname = 'WRBTR' OR
                            fieldname = 'WAERS'.
ENDMETHOD.
```

Listing 2.3 Example — Changing the Field Catalogue

2.3.5 Activating and Deactivating BAdIs

You can activate and deactivate BAdIs in enhancement implementations by following these steps:

1. Select the respective BAdI in the initial screen of the enhancement implementation, and activate or deactivate the implementation by setting or deleting the checkmark for IMPLEMENTATION IS ACTIVE in the RUNTIME BEHAVIOR area (see Figure 2.14).

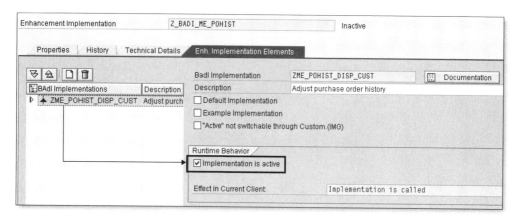

Figure 2.14 Activating or Deactivating the BAdI Implementation

2. If you change the activation status of a BAdI implementation, you must also save and activate the enhancement implementation again (in the example already given, Z_BADI_ME_POHIST).

3   User Exits and BAdIs in Purchasing

Hardly any area of Materials Management (MM) provides as many options to enhance standards as in Purchasing. Deciding which enhancements to present in detail in this chapter wasn't easy. Among the most frequently required and most useful functions are the two enhancements presented in this chapter. Implementing customized fields in the purchase order is a complex topic that leads to many questions, so a large part of this chapter is devoted to exploring these customizations. You can also find an overview of all enhancement options in Appendix A.

3.1   Customized Fields in Purchase Orders

To store custom data together with a purchase order, you must provide the user with the respective input fields. There are various alternatives. The enhancement MM06E005 is provided if you intend to only use a few individual fields at a header or item level. This is relatively simple to implement, and you can directly attach your fields as an append structure to Table EKKO or to Table EKPO. Furthermore, this enhancement is also used in other purchasing documents, for example, in the request for quotation (RFQ), as well as in the classic purchase order transactions.

However, the new method for using customized fields via the BAdIs ME_GUI_PO_ CUST and ME_PROCESS_PO_CUST is described over the next few pages. This method was introduced for Release 4.7. These BAdIs enhance the Enjoy purchase orders; however, the single-screen Transactions ME21N, ME22N, and ME23N provide some benefits here. The BAdIs are more flexible and can also insert more complex requirements seamlessly into the purchase order, and use several custom tabs at the header and item level.

> **Customized Fields in Purchase Requisitions**
>
> For purchase requisitions, the options for implementing custom fields can be compared with those of purchase orders. You can use enhancement MEREQ001 for simple situations and attach the required fields, for example, as an append structure to Table EBAN.

If you require more flexibility, the BAdI `ME_PROCESS_REQ_CUST` is provided, which is similar to the solution presented in this chapter. Therefore, you can transfer the example easily in purchase requisitions

3.1.1 Overview of the Implementation

The implementation of customized fields can be structured essentially into three components. Before going into detail, you should first get an overview of these components.

Part 1 — Encapsulation of Custom Data in a Function Group

A custom function is initially required to include the internal data retention of custom fields, the dynpros in the form of subscreens, and function modules to access the dynpros and the data externally. The integration into the purchase order is executed by calling these function modules from the respective methods of the BAdIs. The necessary function modules are listed in Table 3.1.

Time (Function Module)	Use
Initialize (Z_ME_CUST_INIT)	Deleting the global data, for example, to generate a new document
Open (Z_ME_CUST_OPEN)	Reading the custom data on an already existing purchase order from the database and providing the data in the global data of the function group
Read data (Z_ME_CUST_DATA_GET)	Reading the global data for the header or item and transferring to the calling program
Write data (Z_ME_CUST_DATA_SET)	Writing changed or newly transferred data to global data
Post (Z_ME_CUST_POST)	Calling an update module when the purchase order is saved
Set dynpro (Z_ME_CUST_DYN_SET)	Transferring the data to a dynpro

Table 3.1 Overview of Necessary Function Modules

Time (Function Module)	Use
Read dynpro (Z_ME_CUST_DYN_GET)	Copying the data from a dynpro
Update (Z_ME_CUST_UPDATE)	(Properties: Process type update module): Writing the custom data to the database, the call is executed from the "Post" function module

Table 3.1 Overview of Necessary Function Modules (Cont.)

Part 2 — BAdI MEPO_GUI_PO_CUST

The BAdI MEPO_GUI_PO_CUST includes all methods to insert custom tabs at a header or item level into the purchase order, and to execute the data transport between the function group and the dynpros displayed in the tabstrips. An overview of all the methods is provided in Table 3.2.

Method	Use
SUBSCRIBE	You create new tabstrips (header or item) and assign these to a dynpro of your function group.
MAP_DYNPRO_FIELDS	You map your dynpro fields in a metafield. Metafields describe the content of a dynpro field using various characteristics and are important when notifications are assigned to a specific field, particularly with regard to the display of error messages.
TRANSPORT_FROM_MODEL	This method will run depending on the registered subscreen and its type (header or item). Here you essentially call the Read Data module from your function group. You store the result in a suitable structure in the attributes of your BAdI implementation. You need this data again in the method TRANSPORT_FROM_DYNPRO.
TRANSPORT_TO_DYNPRO	The previously read data is now copied by the call of the Set Dynpro function module to the function group and is then displayed in the dynpro.

Table 3.2 Methods of the BAdI MEPO_GUI_PO_CUST

Method	Use
TRANSPORT_FROM_DYNPRO	After a user has made an entry, you retrieve the data of the dynpro in the BAdI by calling the Read Dynpro function module. Compare the data with the previous status (see TRANSPORT_FROM_MODEL). If the content has changed, you must pass this information to the data model.
TRANSPORT_TO_MODEL	If changes have occurred, you transfer the new data again to your function group by calling the Write Data function module.
EXECUTE	You can use this method optionally to handle custom function codes if you have positioned the respective buttons in a custom dynpro.

Table 3.2 Methods of the BAdI MEPO_GUI_PO_CUST (Cont.)

Part 3 — BAdI MEPO_PROCESS_PO_CUST

The BAdI MEPO_PROCESS_PO_CUST is ultimately used to integrate your custom data into the process flow of the purchase order to execute, for example, input checks and to integrate other function modules from your function group. An overview of these relevant methods is given in Table 3.3

Methods	Use
INITIALIZE	From this method, you call the Initialize function module of your function group when you start your transaction.
OPEN	This method runs as soon as a purchase order is opened. Then you call the Open function module to make custom data available.
PROCESS_ITEM	You can check inputs at item level.
PROCESS_HEADER	You can check inputs at header level.
PROCESS_SCHEDULE	You can check inputs on schedules.
PROCESS_ACCOUNT	You can check inputs for account assignments.
CHECK	This method allows you to check the document completely.

Table 3.3 Methods of the BAdI ME_PROCESS_PO_CUST

Methods	Use
POST	When the purchase order is saved, you must also save your own data by calling the Post function module.
CLOSE	You also call the Initialize function module before a new document is started.
FIELDSELECTION_*	Depending on the context, you can set the field status of your custom fields in various methods for the field selection.

Table 3.3 Methods of the BAdI ME_PROCESS_PO_CUST (Cont.)

Figure 3.1 shows an overview of all the BAdI methods used in the example, as well as their interaction with the custom function group. The SUBSCRIBE, MAP_DYN-PRO_FIELDS, and FIELDSELECT_ITEM methods are necessary to activate the custom fields. However, they don't communicate with your function group.

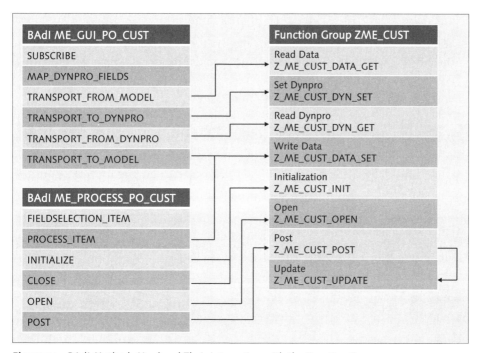

Figure 3.1 BAdI Methods Used and Their Integration with the Function Group

3.1.2 Implementation of Custom Purchase Order Data and Function Group

After you get a general overview of the work involved, the first step is defining custom data and creating the function group. Additional tabs at the header and item levels are integrated with the purchase order so you can enter custom data and save it.

To present the following example in a simpler way, the example only includes the creation of three text fields, respectively, at the header and item level. The data is stored in separate tables. When you understand the principle of BAdIs, you can easily use and store any complex data quantities.

1. Start with the definition of your custom fields in the ABAP Dictionary. Start Transaction SE11, and create a table to store the custom header data (suggestion: ZME_POHEAD). The fields from Table 3.4 are used in the example.

2. Create another table to store the custom item data (suggestion: ZME_POITEM). The fields from Table 3.5 are used in the example.

3. You still require work structures for the dynpros that should also be created in the ABAP Dictionary. Create a structure for the header data (suggestion: ZME_POHEAD_DS) and for the item data, respectively, (suggestion: ZME_POITEM_DS) with the fields from Table 3.6 and Table 3.7.

Field Name	Key Field	Data Element
MANDT	Yes	MANDT
EBELN	Yes	EBELN
ZK_FELD1		CHAR32
ZK_FELD2		CHAR32
ZK_FELD3		CHAR32

Table 3.4 Fields of the Table ZME_POHEAD

Field Name	Key Field	Data Element
MANDT	Yes	MANDT
EBELN	Yes	EBELN

Table 3.5 Fields of the Table ZME_POITEM

Field Name	Key Field	Data Element
EBELP	Yes	EBELP
ZP_FELD1		CHAR32
ZP_FELD2		CHAR32
ZP_FELD3		CHAR32

Table 3.5 Fields of the Table ZME_POITEM (Cont.)

Component	Component Type
ZK_FELD1	CHAR32
ZK_FELD2	CHAR32
ZK_FELD3	CHAR32

Table 3.6 Structure ZME_POHEAD_DS

Component	Component Type
ZP_FELD1	CHAR32
ZP_FELD2	CHAR32
ZP_FELD3	CHAR32

Table 3.7 Structure ZME_POITEM_DS

You've now created the prerequisites necessary in the ABAP Dictionary. The function group can then be created and the dynpros required can be generated.

1. Go to Transaction SE80, and change the object type on the left-hand side in FUNCTION GROUP (see Figure 3.2). Then specify the name of a function group (suggestion: ZME_CUST), and confirm the name by pressing the [Enter] key and confirming the dialog window that appears to create the new function group.

2. Navigate to the include LZME_CUSTTOP to create the global data. Create two structures for the header data and two internal tables with an additional work structure for the item data. Duplicate implementation is used so that an object can always maintain the status of the database, while the other object stores the current content revised by the user. Moreover, you require both ABAP Dictionary structures ZME_POHEAD_DS and ZME_POITEM_DS for the dynpros that you provide with the key term, TABLES.

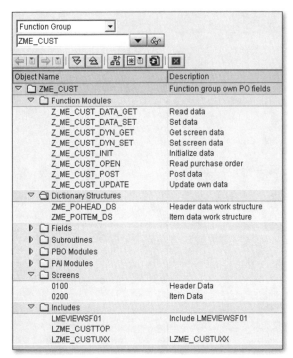

Figure 3.2 Completed Function Group ZME_CUST

3. For the subsequent integration with the purchase order, various standard form routines are called in your program that need to be available. You also integrate the include LMEVIEWSF01. This still requires a global data field OK-CODE to include possible custom function codes. Use Listing 3.1 as a sample.

```
FUNCTION-POOL ZME_CUST.                      "MESSAGE-ID ..

* Dynpro structures
TABLES: zme_pohead_ds,
        zme_poitem_ds.

* Structures for header data
* (_db contains the status of the database)
DATA: gs_pohead_db TYPE zme_pohead,
      gs_pohead    TYPE zme_pohead.

* Table and work structure for the item data
* (_db contains the status of the database)
DATA: gt_poitem_db TYPE SORTED TABLE OF zme_poitem
```

```
                    WITH UNIQUE KEY mandt ebeln ebelp,
      gt_poitem     LIKE gt_poitem_db,
      gs_poitem_db TYPE zme_poitem,
      gs_poitem    TYPE zme_poitem.

* Form routines for dynpro calls. Always necessary!
DATA ok-code TYPE sy-ucomm.
INCLUDE lmeviewsf01.
```
Listing 3.1 Global Data (Include LZME_CUSTTOP)

4. Create a dynpro for the header data in the function group (suggestion: 0100), and insert the three fields from the ABAP Dictionary structure ZME_POHEAD_DS as an input field. Choose the dynpro type in the Subscreen properties.

5. The field properties are controlled via the BAdIs. To interact your dynpro with the BAdIs, you must integrate the modules EVENT_PBO and EVENT_PAI in the flow logic. These modules are also included in the include LMEVIEWSF01 and are already known (see Listing 3.2). Save and activate the dynpro.

```
PROCESS BEFORE OUTPUT.
  MODULE EVENT_PBO.

PROCESS AFTER INPUT.
  MODULE EVENT_PAI.
```
Listing 3.2 Flow Logic for the Dynpros 0100 and 0200

6. Create another dynpro (suggestion: 0200) for the item data. Use the structure ZME_POITEM as a reference here. Proceed as before.

In the next work step, the necessary function modules are created according to Table 3.1.

1. Start with the function module ZME_CUST_INIT to initialize the global data. The module doesn't require any parameters. You can find the coding for this in Listing 3.3.

```
FUNCTION Z_ME_CUST_INIT.
*"----------------------------------------------------------
*"*"Local interface:
*"----------------------------------------------------------

* Initialization of the global data.
```

```
    REFRESH: gt_poitem_db, gt_poitem.
    ClEAR:   gs_pohead_db, gs_pohead,
             gs_poitem_db, gs_poitem,
             zme_pohead_ds, zme_poitem_ds.

ENDFUNCTION.
```
Listing 3.3 Function Module Z_ME_CUST_INIT

2. Create the function module Z_ME_CUST_OPEN to "open" a purchase order. The data is read from the custom database tables and provided in the global data. Only the purchase order number is required as an import parameter. Use Listing 3.4 as a sample.

```
FUNCTION Z_ME_CUST_OPEN.
*"----------------------------------------------------------------
*"*"Local interface:
*"  IMPORTING
*"     REFERENCE(I_EBELN) TYPE  EBELN
*"----------------------------------------------------------------

* Read purchase order header
  SELECT SINGLE * FROM zme_pohead INTO gs_pohead_db
                  WHERE ebeln = i_ebeln.

* Read purchase order items
  SELECT * FROM zme_poitem INTO TABLE gt_poitem_db
                  WHERE ebeln = i_ebeln.

* Copying the database version to the current version
  gs_pohead = gs_pohead_db.
  gt_poitem = gt_poitem_db.
ENDFUNCTION.
```
Listing 3.4 Function Module Z_ME_CUST_OPEN

3. Implement the function module "Read Data". Use Z_ME_CUST_DATA_GET as the name. An import parameter controls whether header data or item data is processed. Two other import parameters specify the document number and the document item. Because the document item is only transferred if necessary, set the OPTIONAL flag for this parameter. You also need the structures of your header and item data as export parameters.

The function module now reads the data from the global area and returns the data via export parameters to the calling program. You can find the respective sample in Listing 3.5.

```
FUNCTION z_me_cust_data_get.
*"----------------------------------------------------------------
*"*"Local interface:
*"  IMPORTING
*"     REFERENCE(I_TYPE) TYPE  STRING
*"     REFERENCE(I_EBELN) TYPE  EBELN
*"     REFERENCE(I_EBELP) TYPE  EBELP OPTIONAL
*"  EXPORTING
*"     REFERENCE(E_HEADER) TYPE  ZME_POHEAD
*"     REFERENCE(E_ITEM) TYPE  ZME_POITEM
*"----------------------------------------------------------------
* I_TYPE: HEADER = header data
*         ITEM   = item data
  CASE i_type.
    WHEN 'HEADER'.
      e_header = gs_pohead.

    WHEN 'ITEM'.
      READ TABLE gt_poitem INTO e_item
                   WITH TABLE KEY mandt = sy-mandt
                                  ebeln = i_ebeln
                                  ebelp = i_ebelp.
      IF sy-subrc NE 0.
*        Item doesn't exist yet, initial data
         CLEAR e_item.
         e_item-mandt = sy-mandt.
         e_item-ebeln = i_ebeln.
         e_item-ebelp = i_ebelp.
      ENDIF.
  ENDCASE.
ENDFUNCTION.
```

Listing 3.5 Function Module Z_ME_CUST_DATA_GET

4. The next step concerns the function module "Write Data". Use the name Z_ME_ CUST_DATA_SET. An import parameter controls whether header data or item data is processed. Define the header and item data also as optional import parameters. Because the structure already contains the purchase order number and the

purchase order item for items, these don't need to be specially transferred. You also need an indicator to define whether an item is to be deleted.

The header data is only overwritten when this function module is called. With regard to the item data, first check whether this item already exists in the internal table to overwrite the line if required or to insert a new line in the table. If the deletion indicator is set, remove the line from the internal table. You can view the sample in Listing 3.6.

```
FUNCTION z_me_cust_data_set.
*"----------------------------------------------------------
*"*"Local interface:
*"  IMPORTING
*"     REFERENCE(I_TYPE) TYPE  STRING
*"     REFERENCE(I_HEADER) TYPE  ZME_POHEAD OPTIONAL
*"     REFERENCE(I_ITEM) TYPE  ZME_POITEM OPTIONAL
*"     REFERENCE(I_DELKZ) TYPE  XFELD OPTIONAL
*"----------------------------------------------------------

* I_TYPE: HEADER = Header data
*         ITEM   = Item data
  CASE i_type.
    WHEN 'HEADER'.
      gs_pohead = i_header.

    WHEN 'ITEM'.
*     Delete item?
      IF i_delkz IS NOT INITIAL.
        DELETE TABLE gt_poitem
             WITH TABLE KEY mandt = sy-mandt
                            ebeln = i_item-ebeln
                            ebelp = i_item-ebelp.
      ELSE.
        CLEAR gs_poitem.

*       Item already available?
        READ TABLE gt_poitem INTO gs_poitem
             WITH TABLE KEY mandt = sy-mandt
                            ebeln = i_item-ebeln
                            ebelp = i_item-ebelp.
        IF sy-subrc = 0.
*         Update line
          gs_poitem = i_item.
```

```
              gs_poitem-mandt = sy-mandt.
              MODIFY gt_poitem FROM gs_poitem INDEX sy-tabix.
           ELSE.
*          Insert line
              gs_poitem = i_item.
              gs_poitem-mandt = sy-mandt.
              INSERT gs_poitem INTO TABLE gt_poitem.
           ENDIF.
        ENDIF.
   ENDCASE.
ENDFUNCTION.
```

Listing 3.6 Function Module Z_ME_CUST_DATA_SET

5. You also need two other function modules for the communication with the dynpros: Z_ME_CUST_DYN_SET and Z_ME_CUST_DYN_GET. A respective import parameter is again required to distinguish between header and item data.

▶ For Z_ME_CUST_DYN_SET, create two structures for the header or item data (type ZME_POHEAD_DS and ZME_POITEM_DS) as further import parameters. Set the OPTIONAL flag again because only header or item data are transferred.

▶ To retrieve data via the function module Z_ME_CUST_DYN_GET, set up the respective export parameters for the associated data ZME_POHEAD_DS and ZME_POITEM_DS.

You can view the coding for both modules in Listing 3.7 and Listing 3.8.

```
FUNCTION z_me_cust_dyn_get.
*"----------------------------------------------------------------
*"*"Local interface:
*"  IMPORTING
*"     REFERENCE(I_TYPE) TYPE  STRING
*"  EXPORTING
*"     REFERENCE(E_POHEAD) TYPE  ZME_POHEAD_DS
*"     REFERENCE(E_POITEM) TYPE  ZME_POITEM_DS
*"----------------------------------------------------------------

* I_TYPE: HEADER = header data
*         ITEM   = Item data
  CASE i_type.
    WHEN 'HEADER'.
      e_pohead = zme_pohead_ds.
    WHEN 'ITEM'.
      e_poitem = zme_poitem_ds.
```

```
      ENDCASE.
   ENDFUNCTION.
```

Listing 3.7 Function Module Z_ME_CUST_DYN_GET

```
FUNCTION z_me_cust_dyn_set.
*"----------------------------------------------------------
*"*"Local interface:
*"  IMPORTING
*"     REFERENCE(I_TYPE) TYPE  STRING
*"     REFERENCE(I_POHEAD) TYPE  ZME_POHEAD_DS OPTIONAL
*"     REFERENCE(I_POITEM) TYPE  ZME_POITEM_DS OPTIONAL
*"----------------------------------------------------------
* I_TYPE: HEADER = Header data
*         ITEM  = Item data
   CASE i_type.
     WHEN 'HEADER'.
       zme_pohead_ds = i_pohead.
     WHEN 'ITEM'.
       zme_poitem_ds = i_poitem.
   ENDCASE.
ENDFUNCTION.
```

Listing 3.8 Function Module Z_ME_CUST_DYN_SET

Both modules are ultimately required for updating. A module formats the data and then transfers it to the second module, which is an update module.

1. Create the module Z_ME_CUST_UPDATE and activate the option UPDATE MODULE for this in the properties in the PROCESSING TYPE section. To avoid any unnecessary accesses to the database, the header and item data are transferred twice to this module: Once in the status on how it is found in the database (that you have parked, refer to Listings 3.1 and 3.4) and once in the current status revised by the user.

2. The internal tables with the items are transferred in the example as table parameters. When the tables are to be transferred as CHANGING parameters, you must first create another table type in the ABAP Dictionary. Because it's an update module, you must set the PASS VALUE flag for the import parameters.

3. The two statuses must be compared, and only when a difference exists must the line be inserted into, or be updated in, the database tables. Listing 3.9 includes the example for this module.

```
FUNCTION z_me_cust_update.
*"----------------------------------------------------------
*"*"Local interface:
*"  IMPORTING
*"     REFERENCE(I_POHEAD_DB) TYPE  ZME_POHEAD
*"     REFERENCE(I_POHEAD) TYPE  ZME_POHEAD
*"  TABLES
*"     T_POITEM_DB STRUCTURE  ZME_POITEM
*"     T_POITEM STRUCTURE  ZME_POITEM
*"----------------------------------------------------------

  DATA: lt_item_new TYPE TABLE OF zme_poitem,
        lt_item_chg TYPE TABLE OF zme_poitem.

* Update of the header data.
  IF i_pohead_db IS INITIAL.
*   Header data aren't yet in the DB
    INSERT zme_pohead FROM i_pohead.
  ELSE.
    IF i_pohead_db <> i_pohead.
*     Data have been changed
      UPDATE zme_pohead FROM i_pohead.
    ENDIF.
  ENDIF.

* Preparing the item data
  LOOP AT t_poitem INTO gs_poitem.
*   Was this line there previously?
    READ TABLE t_poitem_db INTO gs_poitem_db
             WITH KEY mandt = sy-mandt
                      ebeln = gs_poitem-ebeln
                      ebelp = gs_poitem-ebelp.
    IF sy-subrc = 0.
*     Item was already in DB, delete and
*     note if applicable
      DELETE t_poitem_db INDEX sy-tabix.

      IF gs_poitem_db <> gs_poitem.
*       Content changed, note for UPDATE
        APPEND gs_poitem TO lt_item_chg.
      ENDIF.
    ELSE.
*     Item is new, note for Insert
```

51

```
      APPEND gs_poitem TO lt_item_new.
    ENDIF.
  ENDLOOP.


* Updating the item data
* 1. New lines
  IF lt_item_new IS NOT INITIAL.
    INSERT zme_poitem FROM TABLE lt_item_new.
  ENDIF.


* 2. Changed lines
  IF lt_item_chg IS NOT INITIAL.
    UPDATE zme_poitem FROM TABLE lt_item_chg.
  ENDIF.


* 3. Lines that are now still in t_poitem_db
* can still be found in the database , haven't however
* been retransferred -> conclusion: The lines
* have been deleted by the user ...
  IF t_poitem_db[] IS NOT INITIAL.
    DELETE zme_poitem FROM TABLE t_poitem_db.
  ENDIF.
ENDFUNCTION.
```

Listing 3.9 Function Module Z_ME_CUST_UPDATE

4. Create the module Z_ME_CUST_POST, which prepares the data for updating and calls the previously created function module Z_ME_CUST_UPDATE with the addition IN UPDATE TASK.

5. You need an import parameter with the document number. This document number is only provided with new documents during the posting and is then transferred to the function module via this parameter. You must also enhance the client in the update data or the comparison to changes will fail. Copy the document number in the structure with the header data and in the internal table with the items. Then transfer the formatted data to the update module.

Caution

Under no circumstances should you trigger (as well as in any other position within the entire enhancement) a COMMIT WORK — this is only performed by the SAP standard coding!

You can find the sample in Listing 3.10.

```
FUNCTION z_me_cust_post.
*"----------------------------------------------------------
*"*"Local interface:
*"  IMPORTING
*"     REFERENCE(I_EBELN) TYPE  EKKO-EBELN
*"----------------------------------------------------------
  FIELD-SYMBOLS <fs_item> TYPE zme_poitem.
  DATA: ls_pohead_db TYPE zme_pohead,
        ls_pohead    TYPE zme_pohead,
        lt_poitem_db TYPE TABLE OF zme_poitem,
        lt_poitem    TYPE TABLE OF zme_poitem.

* No update without document number!
  CHECK i_ebeln IS NOT INITIAL.

* Create and change local copy
  ls_pohead_db = gs_pohead_db.
  ls_pohead    = gs_pohead.
  lt_poitem_db = gt_poitem_db.
  lt_poitem    = gt_poitem.

* Enhance new header data
  ls_pohead-mandt = sy-mandt.
  ls_pohead-ebeln = i_ebeln.
* Enhance new item data
  LOOP AT lt_poitem ASSIGNING <fs_item>.
    <fs_item>-mandt = sy-mandt.
    <fs_item>-ebeln = i_ebeln.
  ENDLOOP.

* Calling the update module
  CALL FUNCTION 'Z_ME_CUST_UPDATE'
    IN UPDATE TASK
    EXPORTING
      i_pohead_db = ls_pohead_db
      i_pohead    = ls_pohead
    TABLES
      t_poitem_db = lt_poitem_db
      t_poitem    = lt_poitem.
ENDFUNCTION.
```

Listing 3.10 Function Module Z_ME_CUST_POST

3.1.3   Integration of Custom Fields into the BAdIs

Now the entire data administration of your custom fields is complete. However, these fields still need to be integrated with the Enjoy transactions for the purchase order (ME21N, ME22N, and ME23N). This is relatively simple for the header data. Some methods are additionally required for the item data to send a message to your function group if the user has navigated between the items.

The next milestone is to integrate your new dynpros in custom tabstrips with the purchase order even if they still don't have any function. Three prerequisites must be fulfilled for this.

▶ The tabstrips must be specified via the method SUBSCRIBE of the BAdI ME_GUI_PO_CUST.

▶ The fields that can be found in your previously defined dynpros must be linked to a metafield via the MAP_DYNPRO_FIELDS method of the same BAdI.

▶ At least one field in the dynpros must be displayed. Without any further action, your fields will only appear in the display transaction ME23N. These fields are hidden when they are created or changed. You also won't see any tabstrip in this case. To prevent this, you must additionally use the FIELDSELECTION_HEADER and FIELDSELECTION_ITEM methods of the BAdI ME_PROCESS_PO_CUST and fundamentally display your fields.

Using these methods isn't as complex as it may look. Follow these steps to proceed:

1. Create an implementation for the BAdI ME_GUI_PO_CUST as well as for the BAdI ME_PROCESS_PO_CUST. Methods from both BAdI implementations will now be required repeatedly.

2. The method SUBSCRIBE is important. All custom tabstrips are specified in it and linked with a custom dynpro. The method has three parameters:

   ▶ The IM_APPLICATION parameter displays from which application the BAdI has been called. This is currently always filled with PO because the BAdI is only integrated into the purchase order. To be on the safe side, however, you can implement a query in this value.

▶ The IM_ELEMENT parameter either contains HEADER or ITEM as a value depending on whether the call is executed for the header or item level.

▶ Depending on this value, you must populate the third parameter, RE_SUB-SCRIBERS, which is an internal table. You can see its structure in Table 3.8.

Table Field	Description
NAME	A unique identification of the tabstrip of type MEPO_NAME. Using this name, you can recognize which dynpro is currently being run in other methods of the BAdI.
DYNPRO	The number of your own dynpro.
PROGRAM	The program in which your custom dynpro is located.
STRUCT_NAME	An ABAP Dictionary structure that describes your custom fields in this dynpro.
LABEL	The title given to the tabstrip in the transaction.
POSITION	The item of the tabstrip. If you enter the value 3 here, for example, the tabstrip appears in the third position from left.
HEIGHT	The height of the tabstrip. Only two values are currently interpreted here: A value less than or equal to 7 results in a tabstrip with a height of seven lines. A value greater than 7 results in a tabstrip with a height of 16 lines.

Table 3.8 Description of the Parameter RE_SUBSCRIBERS

3. You'll require the unique identification of the tabstrip that you must assign to the field NAME (see Table 3.8) in several methods. You should therefore define these in the attributes of the implementing class as constants — you can access the attributes of the class from all methods. To do this, open the implementation of the BAdI ME_GUI_PO_CUST. Double-click the name of the implementing class (ZCL_IM_ME_GUI_PO_CUST), and switch to the ATTRIBUTES tabstrip.

4. Create a constant of the type MEPO_NAME, which contains the programmed name of your tabstrip and item tabstrip (see Figure 3.3). Then register your dynpros. You can find the sample in Listing 3.11.

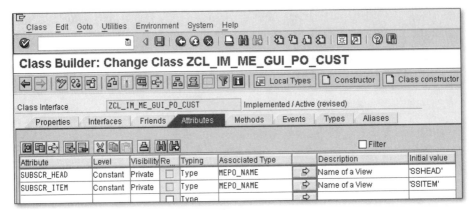

Figure 3.3 Attributes of the Implementing Class

```
METHOD if_ex_me_gui_po_cust~subscribe.
  DATA: ls_subscriber LIKE LINE OF re_subscribers.

* Only from the purchase order (currently always 'PO', therefore only
* to be on the safe side)
  CHECK im_application = 'PO'.
  REFRESH re_subscribers.

* Depending on whether header or item tabstrips
* are required to register custom dynpros
  CASE im_element.
    WHEN 'HEADER'.
      ls_subscriber-name = subscr_head.

*       Dynpro from custom function group:
        ls_subscriber-dynpro      = '0100'.
        ls_subscriber-program     = 'SAPLZME_CUST'.
        ls_subscriber-struct_name = 'ZME_POHEAD_DS'.

*       Caption of the tabstrip
        ls_subscriber-label   = 'Eigene Daten'(001).

*       Position and height
        ls_subscriber-position = 1.
        ls_subscriber-height   = 7.
        APPEND ls_subscriber TO re_subscribers.
    WHEN 'ITEM'.
      ls_subscriber-name = subscr_item.
```

```
*       Dynpro from custom function group:
        ls_subscriber-dynpro       = '0200'.
        ls_subscriber-program      = 'SAPLZME_CUST'.
        ls_subscriber-struct_name = 'ZME_POITEM_DS'.

*       Caption of the tabstrip
        ls_subscriber-label      = 'Eigene Daten'(001).

*       Position and height
        ls_subscriber-position = 99.
        ls_subscriber-height   = 7.
        APPEND ls_subscriber TO re_subscribers.
    ENDCASE.
ENDMETHOD.
```

Listing 3.11 Method SUBSCRIBE from ME_GUI_PO_CUST

The fields of your dynpros must then be assigned to the metafields. This takes place in method MAP_DYNPRO_FIELDS of the ME_GUI_PO_CUST BAdI. This method only has an internal table CH_MAPPING as a parameter that contains all fields you've redefined. You can query the respective field via the table column FIELDNAME. Here you must assign each field via the METAFIELD table column.

Metafields have the data type MMPUR_METAFIELD, which ultimately displays only one integer value. Values from 90000000 and above are reserved for customers. In the MMMFD type group, there are 10 predefined customer metafields that you can use. These are the fields MMMFD_CUST_01 (90000000) to MMMFD_CUST_10 (90000009). If you require more fields, you can create more in a custom type group.

You can see how a predefined metafield is assigned using the following steps:

1. Open the implementation of the ME_GUI_PO_CUST BAdI, and navigate again to the implementing class (ZCL_IM_ME_GUI_PO_CUST).

2. In the PROPERTIES tabstrip, you must now specify the type group MMMFD by entering this on the right-hand side in the FORWARD DECLARATIONS area (see Figure 3.4).

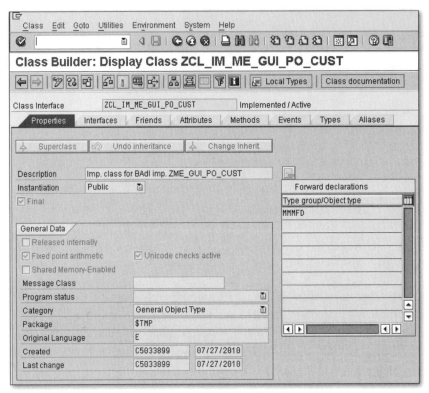

Figure 3.4 Definition of the Type Group as a Forward Declaration

3. Go to the MAP_DYNPRO_FIELDS method, and assign a metafield to the fields of the dynpros. For the fields ZK_FELD1 to ZK_FELD3, use the metafields MMMFD_CUST_01 to MMMFD_CUST_03, and for the fields ZP_FELD1 to ZP_FELD3, take the metafields MMMFD_CUST_04 to MMMFD_CUST_06. Use Listing 3.12 as a template.

```
METHOD if_ex_me_gui_po_cust~map_dynpro_fields.
  FIELD-SYMBOLS: <mapping> LIKE LINE OF ch_mapping.

  LOOP AT ch_mapping ASSIGNING <mapping>.
    CASE <mapping>-fieldname.
*     Map header fields
      WHEN 'ZK_FELD1'.
        <mapping>-metafield = mmmfd_cust_01.
      WHEN 'ZK_FELD2'.
        <mapping>-metafield = mmmfd_cust_02.
      WHEN 'ZK_FELD3'.
        <mapping>-metafield = mmmfd_cust_03.
```

```
*       Map item fields
        WHEN 'ZP_FELD1'.
          <mapping>-metafield = mmmfd_cust_04.
        WHEN 'ZP_FELD2'.
          <mapping>-metafield = mmmfd_cust_05.
        WHEN 'ZP_FELD3'.
          <mapping>-metafield = mmmfd_cust_06.
    ENDCASE.
  ENDLOOP.
ENDMETHOD.
```

Listing 3.12 *Method MAP_DYNPRO_FIELDS from ME_GUI_PO_CUST*

If you activate your BAdIs, you can view the new tabstrips in Transaction ME23N. However, the tabstrip isn't yet displayed when created or in the change mode because the fields are hidden in this case. To set the field status correctly, you still need the methods FIELDSELECTION_HEADER and FIELDSELECTION_ITEM of the BAdI ME_PROCESS_PO_CUST.

The internal table CH_FIELDSELECTION consists of two columns. The METAFIELD column contains the metafield that you assigned to a dynpro field in the previous step. You can overwrite the FIELDSTATUS field with the desired status using Table 3.9.

Status	Explanation
-	Hidden field (when you hide all fields, the tabstrip is also hidden)
*	Display field
.	Input field
+	Mandatory field

Table 3.9 Field Status — Overview of Options

You can also access the data model of the header data via the IM_HEADER parameter (reference to the interface IF_PURCHASE_ORDER_MM). The IM_ITEM parameter (reference to the interface IF_PURCHASE_ORDER_ITEM_MM) also exists for the items. Various methods are provided for the interfaces to obtain information on the content and status of the purchase order. You can directly view the interfaces in Transaction SE24.

As an example, the fields in the purchase order display should only be display fields. However, a ready-for-input status is desired in the change mode. The header field ZK_FELD3 should only become ready for input when the header of the purchase order does not contain any errors. To make this happen, implement the following steps:

1. Open your implementation for the ME_PROCESS_PO_CUST BAdI. Navigate to the implementing class (ZCL_IM_ME_PROCESS_PO_CUST), and insert the MMMFD type group.

2. Program the FIELDSELECTION_HEADER and FIELDSELECTION_ITEM methods according to the description. You can find the methods in Listing 3.13 and Listing 3.14, respectively.

```
METHOD if_ex_me_process_po_cust~fieldselection_header.
  FIELD-SYMBOLS <chfs> TYPE mmpur_fs.
  DATA lv_changeable TYPE mmpur_bool.

* Can the purchase order be changed (create/change)?
  lv_changeable = im_header->is_changeable( ).

* Override field selection
  LOOP AT ch_fieldselection ASSIGNING <chfs>.
    IF lv_changeable IS INITIAL.
*       Display mode, field is not supposed to be ready for input
      <chfs>-fieldstatus = '*'.
    ELSE.

*     Field is to be ready for input
      <chfs>-fieldstatus = '.'.
    ENDIF.

*   Special rule for field ZK_FELD3 (detection via metafield):
*   Hide, so long as header of the purchase order contains errors
    IF <chfs>-metafield = mmmfd_cust_03.
      IF im_header->is_valid( ) IS INITIAL.
        <chfs>-fieldstatus = '-'.
      ENDIF.
    ENDIF.
  ENDLOOP.
ENDMETHOD.
```

Listing 3.13 Method FIELDSELECTION_HEADER of ME_PROCESS_PO_CUST

```
METHOD if_ex_me_process_po_cust~fieldselection_item.
  FIELD-SYMBOLS <chfs> TYPE mmpur_fs.
  DATA lv_changeable TYPE mmpur_bool.

* Can the purchase order be changed (create/change)?
  lv_changeable = im_header->is_changeable( ).

* Override field selection
  LOOP AT ch_fieldselection ASSIGNING <chfs>.
    IF lv_changeable IS INITIAL.
*     Display mode, field isn't supposed to be ready for input
      <chfs>-fieldstatus = '*'.
    ELSE.
*     Field is supposed to be ready for input
      <chfs>-fieldstatus = '.'.
    ENDIF.
  ENDLOOP.
ENDMETHOD.
```

Listing 3.14 Method FIELDSELECTION_ITEM of ME_PROCESS_PO_CUST

3.1.4 Integration of Customer Fields into the Business Logic

The dynpros have now been successfully integrated into the purchase order. However, the integration into the business logic of the purchase order is still missing. Above all, the correct data must be retrieved from the data model at the correct time and added to the dynpros. When changes are made, this data must be copied back from the dynpro to the data model. Correct handling is important, particularly for the items, because other data is supposed to be made visible in the dynpro for every item here.

In the ME_GUI_PO_CUST BAdI, the process for each defined tabstrip is specified as follows:

1. TRANSPORT_FROM_MODEL
   Here you read the custom data to be displayed in the dynpro from the data model (your function group) and temporarily save this in an attribute of your implementing class.

2. TRANSPORT_TO_DYNP
   The previously retrieved data must be transferred to the structure, the fields of which are displayed in the dynpro. The dynpro is now displayed and can be edited by the user.

3. TRANSPORT_FROM_DYNP

Now retrieve the data again from the dynpro structure, and save the result in a second attribute of your implementing class. Compare whether there has been a change to the data in comparison to the status in Step 1. If so, check the RE_CHANGED flag.

4. TRANSPORT_TO_MODEL

This method is only called if you have set the RE_CHANGED flag in Step 3. Transport the changed data here back to your function group.

In each method, obtain the name of the tabstrip previously defined in the SUB-SCRIBE method via the IM_NAME parameter. The data of the purchase order is also provided in a reference in the data model as the IM_MODEL parameter. Using this reference, you obtain the header data via the interface IF_PURCHASE_ORDER_MM and the item data via the interface IF_PURCHASE_ORDER_ITEM_MM.

To access this data, create a local reference in one of the two interfaces, and then implement an upcast from the transferred data model. To do this, you can use the MMPUR_DYNAMIC_CAST macro. You access the respective interfaces as follows:

```
DATA: l_header    TYPE REF TO if_purchase_order_mm,
      l_item      TYPE REF TO if_purchase_order_item_mm.
mmpur_dynamic_cast l_header im_model.
mmpur_dynamic_cast l_item im_model.
```

You are now provided with all methods of both interfaces via L_HEADER or L_ITEM. The most important method might be GET_DATA, through which you access the fields of the purchase order. You can find out again about further methods and their respective parameters for these interfaces directly via Transaction SE24.

Interfaces and Upcasts

The interface and upcast concepts come from object-oriented programming. An interface describes an object in the form of attributes and methods. However, it doesn't contain any implementation, and the methods therefore don't contain any coding. A class can now refer to an interface. In this case, the class must implement all attributes and methods defined in the interface and program the methods. The class may also implement other interfaces or contain additional custom attributes and methods. The class is therefore more detailed than the original interface.

You can create a local object with reference to an interface and assign the object of the class (an object is an instance of a class). In this case, the assigned object contains more information than your local object. Therefore, only part of the object defined in the interface is copied. The navigation from one detailed object to a less detailed object is referred to as an upcast.

The advantage of an interface is that only the interface must be specified to users (in this case, you). You don't need to know what the object is and what other information this object contains. You simply retrieve the part relevant to you from the object via the interface and the upcast.

An upcast is implemented via the assignment operator (?=). You can, however, use the MMPUR_DYNAMIC_CAST macro in this BAdI, which also contains error handling.

Let's implement this information in practice:

1. Navigate to your implementation for the ME_GUI_PO_CUST BAdI, go to the implementing class, and then navigate to the ATTRIBUTES tabstrip. Create four private instance attributes: GS_HEADER_PBO and GS_HEADER_PAI of type ZME_POHEAD, as well as GS_ITEM_PBO and GS_ITEM_PAI of type ZME_POITEM (see Figure 3.5).

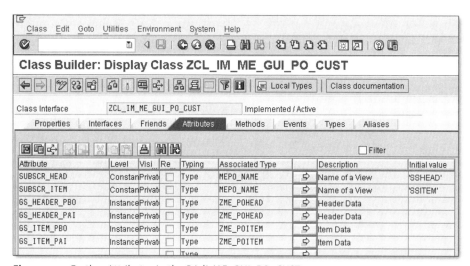

Figure 3.5 Further Attributes in the BAdI ME_GUI_PO_CUST

2. Navigate to the TRANSPORT_FROM_MODEL method, retrieve the current values from your function group depending on the tabstrip displayed, and save these in the GS_HEADER_PBO or GS_ITEM_PBO attribute (see Listing 3.15).

```
METHOD if_ex_me_gui_po_cust~transport_from_model.
   DATA: l_header     TYPE REF TO if_purchase_order_mm,
         l_item       TYPE REF TO if_purchase_order_item_mm.

   DATA: ls_mepoheader TYPE mepoheader,
         ls_mepoitem   TYPE mepoitem.
```

```
    CASE im_name.
      WHEN subscr_head.
*       Header tabstrip, retrieve reference in header data
        mmpur_dynamic_cast l_header im_model.
        CHECK l_header IS NOT INITIAL.
        ls_mepoheader = l_header->get_data( ).

*       Retrieve current header data from model, and note
*        in gs_header_pbo attribute
        CALL FUNCTION 'Z_ME_CUST_DATA_GET'
          EXPORTING
            i_type  = 'HEADER'
            i_ebeln = ls_mepoheader-ebeln
          IMPORTING
            e_header = gs_header_pbo.

      WHEN subscr_item.
*       Item tabstrip, retrieve reference in item data
        mmpur_dynamic_cast l_item im_model.
        CHECK l_item IS NOT INITIAL.
        ls_mepoitem = l_item->get_data( ).

*       Retrieve current item data from model, and
*       note in gs_item_pbo attribute
        CALL FUNCTION 'Z_ME_CUST_DATA_GET'
          EXPORTING
            i_type  = 'ITEM'
            i_ebeln = ls_mepoitem-ebeln
            i_ebelp = ls_mepoitem-ebelp
          IMPORTING
            e_item  = gs_item_pbo.

    ENDCASE.
ENDMETHOD.
```

Listing 3.15 Method TRANSPORT_FROM_MODEL

3. The TRANSPORT_TO_DYNP method must be created in the next step. Depending on the tabstrip used, create a local structure for your dynpro structure, and copy the relevant fields from the previously parked GS_HEADER_PBO and GS_ITEM_PBO attributes. Transfer this structure to the dynpro of your function group so that

the data contained in the structure is displayed there when the dynpro is called (see Listing 3.16).

```
METHOD if_ex_me_gui_po_cust~transport_to_dynp.
* Local copies of the dynpro structures
  DATA: ls_head_ds TYPE zme_pohead_ds,
        ls_item_ds TYPE zme_poitem_ds.

  CASE im_name.
    WHEN subscr_head.
*      Fill  header data, Dynpro structure...
       MOVE-CORRESPONDING gs_header_pbo TO ls_head_ds.

*      ... and transfer
       CALL FUNCTION 'Z_ME_CUST_DYN_SET'
         EXPORTING
           i_type  = 'HEADER'
           i_pohead = ls_head_ds.

    WHEN subscr_item.
*      Fill item data, dynpro structure ...
       MOVE-CORRESPONDING gs_item_pbo TO ls_item_ds.

*      ... and transfer
       CALL FUNCTION 'Z_ME_CUST_DYN_SET'
         EXPORTING
           i_type  = 'ITEM'
           i_poitem = ls_item_ds.
  ENDCASE.
ENDMETHOD.
```
Listing 3.16 Method TRANSPORT_TO_DYNP

4. Now focus on the TRANSPORT_FROM_DYNP method, and retrieve the data here once again from the dynpro. Copy the data to the GS_HEADER_PAI or GS_ITEM_PAI structure for comparison. Compare whether there have been any changes to the data, and if necessary, set the RE_CHANGED flag (see Listing 3.17).

```
METHOD if_ex_me_gui_po_cust~transport_from_dynp.
* Local copies of the dynpro structures
  DATA: ls_head_ds TYPE zme_pohead_ds,
        ls_item_ds TYPE zme_poitem_ds.
```

```
    CASE im_name.
      WHEN subscr_head.
*        Retrieve header data, dynpro data...
         CALL FUNCTION 'Z_ME_CUST_DYN_GET'
           EXPORTING
             i_type   = 'HEADER'
           IMPORTING
             e_pohead = ls_head_ds.

*        ... and copy back
         gs_header_pai = gs_header_pbo.
         MOVE-CORRESPONDING ls_head_ds TO gs_header_pai.

      WHEN subscr_item.
*        Retrieve  item data, Dynpro data...
         CALL FUNCTION 'Z_ME_CUST_DYN_GET'
           EXPORTING
             i_type   = 'ITEM'
           IMPORTING
             e_poitem = ls_item_ds.

*        ... and copy back
         gs_item_pai = gs_item_pbo.
         MOVE-CORRESPONDING ls_item_ds TO gs_item_pai.
    ENDCASE.

* Has the user changed data?
    IF gs_header_pbo <> gs_header_pai OR
       gs_item_pbo    <> gs_item_pai.
*     set flag
      re_changed = 'X'.
    ENDIF.
ENDMETHOD.
```
Listing 3.17 Method TRANSPORT_FROM_DYNP

5. You must now copy possible changes to the TRANSPORT_TO_MODEL method back to your function group. You have already saved the new data in the GS_HEADER_PAI and GS_ITEM_PAI attributes. You must therefore copy the data back to the function group only via the already existing function modules.

If you open an existing purchase order and then only change custom data and want to save the purchase order again, you'll get the message "No data has been

changed." To avoid this, you need to announce the data change. The TRANS-
PORT_TO_MODEL method will only run if custom data has been changed. This
method can therefore be used to announce the change. For this, retrieve the
IF_PURCHASE_ORDER_MM interface, and call the SET_CHANGED method there. The
complete example is shown in Listing 3.18.

```
METHOD if_ex_me_gui_po_cust~transport_to_model.
  DATA: l_header     TYPE REF TO if_purchase_order_mm.

* Inform model that data has been changed
  mmpur_dynamic_cast l_header im_model.
  l_header->set_changed( ).

  CASE im_name.
    WHEN subscr_head.
*      Copy back header data to model
      CALL FUNCTION 'Z_ME_CUST_DATA_SET'
        EXPORTING
          i_type   = 'HEADER'
          i_header = gs_header_pai.

    WHEN subscr_item.
*      Copy back item data to model
      CALL FUNCTION 'Z_ME_CUST_DATA_SET'
        EXPORTING
          i_type = 'ITEM'
          i_item = gs_item_pai.
  ENDCASE.
ENDMETHOD.
```

Listing 3.18 Method TRANSPORT_TO_MODEL

6. The data transport is now completed. You still need to handle one situation,
however. If the user deletes a line of the purchase order, the associated custom
data should also be removed in the data model. When a line is deleted, none of
the previously mentioned methods will run. Therefore, this case must be handled in the PROCESS_ITEM method of the ME_PROCESS_PO_CUST BAdI. Here the
reference in the IF_PURCHASE_ORDER_ITEM_MM interface is directly transferred as
the IM_ITEM parameter. Therefore, an upcast isn't required. With the GET_DATA
method, you must only retrieve and check the data to determine whether the
deletion indicator (LOEKZ) is set (see Listing 3.19).

```
METHOD if_ex_me_process_po_cust~process_item.
  DATA: ls_mepoitem TYPE mepoitem.
  DATA: ls_item TYPE zme_poitem.

* Retrieve item data
  ls_mepoitem = im_item->get_data( ).

* Is the deletion indicator set?
  IF ls_mepoitem-loekz = 'D'.
*    Deleted item
      ls_item-ebeln = ls_mepoitem-ebeln.
      ls_item-ebelp = ls_mepoitem-ebelp.

    CALL FUNCTION 'Z_ME_CUST_DATA_SET'
      EXPORTING
        i_type  = 'ITEM'
        i_item  = ls_item
        i_delkz = 'X'.
  ENDIF.
ENDMETHOD.
```

Listing 3.19 *Method PROCESS_ITEM from ME_PROCESS_PO_CUST*

3.1.5 Initializing, Reading, and Updating Data

To complete the enhancement, only a few more calls in the function group are now necessary. The custom data must be initialized when the purchase order transaction is started or a purchase order is closed. Moreover, the data from the database needs to be read as soon as an existing purchase order is opened. Finally, you need to activate the update of your own data when you save the purchase order.

1. Process the INITIALIZE (initialization of the purchase order transactions) and CLOSE (exiting a purchase order) methods of the ME_PROCESS_PO_CUST BAdI, and initialize your own data from here by calling the function module Z_ME_CUST_INIT (see Listing 3.20 and Listing 3.21).

2. Navigate to the OPEN method, and then call your function module Z_ME_CUST_OPEN to read the custom data. To do this, you only have to transfer the purchase order number, which you obtain again via the GET_DATA method of the IM_HEADER reference parameter (see Listing 3.22).

3. To update the data, you now need the POST method of the BAdI in which you call your function module Z_ME_CUST_POST. This also requires the document

number, which is directly transferred here in the `IM_EBELN` parameter (see Listing 3.23).

```
METHOD if_ex_me_process_po_cust~initialize.
* Initialize custom data
  CALL FUNCTION 'Z_ME_CUST_INIT'.
ENDMETHOD.
```

Listing 3.20 Method INITIALIZE of ME_PROCESS_PO_CUST

```
METHOD if_ex_me_process_po_cust~close.
* Initialize custom data
  CALL FUNCTION 'Z_ME_CUST_INIT'.
ENDMETHOD.
```

Listing 3.21 Method CLOSE of ME_PROCESS_PO_CUST

```
METHOD if_ex_me_process_po_cust~open.
  DATA: ls_mepoheader TYPE mepoheader.

* Retrieve header data /Belegnummer
  ls_mepoheader = im_header->get_data( ).

* Read custom data on purchase order number.
  CALL FUNCTION 'Z_ME_CUST_OPEN'
    EXPORTING
      i_ebeln = ls_mepoheader-ebeln.
ENDMETHOD.
```

Listing 3.22 Method OPEN of ME_PROCESS_PO_CUST

```
METHOD if_ex_me_process_po_cust~post.
* Update custom data
  CALL FUNCTION 'Z_ME_CUST_POST'
    EXPORTING
      i_ebeln = im_ebeln.
ENDMETHOD.
```

Listing 3.23 Method POST of ME_PROCESS_PO_CUST

3.1.6   Display of Error Messages

You are likely planning to carry out input checks for your own fields sooner or later and to display warning or error messages. The Enjoy purchase order transactions use a message collector for messages; that is, messages are not directly displayed but are first collected, and then displayed as an overview upon request (see Figure 3.6).

Figure 3.6 Messages via the Message Collector

Furthermore, you can mark notifications in this window, and navigate directly to the relevant input field via EDIT. To do this, you must link the message with a metafield (that shows a dynpro element).

You can perform your input check in one of the methods listed in Table 3.10. Add the MM_MESSAGES_MAC include, which includes some macros, and which you can use to display messages very simply and execute the required metafield connections. You then display messages as follows:

1. Use the MMPUR_METAFIELD macro to refer to subsequent messages in a specific metafield:

   ```
   mmpur_metafield mmmfd_cust_01.
   ```

2. Submit a message with the MMPUR_MESSAGE_FORCED macro to the message collector. Transfer sequentially the message type, message class, message number, and the placeholders 1-4:

   ```
   mmpur_message_forced 'W' 'ZME' '001'
      'msgv1' 'msgv2' 'msgv3' 'msgv4'.
   ```

3. If the posting of the purchase order is supposed to be prevented until the errors have been resolved, you must set the corresponding status yourself. This happens when you call the INVALIDATE method provided in all methods from Table 3.10 via the model (IM_HEADER, IM_ITEM, IM_SCHEDULE or IM_ACCOUNT parameters).

Method	Description
PROCESS_HEADER	Processing of the header data
PROCESS_ITEM	Processing of the item data
PROCESS_SCHEDULE	Processing of scheduling data
PROCESS_ACCOUNT	Processing of account assignment data
CHECK	Closing checks complete document

Table 3.10 Methods for the Input Check

Listing 3.24 provides a simple example of an input check. The ZK_FELD2 field from the header data of the purchase order must have the content "1" or "2" so that the purchase order may be posted.

```
METHOD if_ex_me_process_po_cust~process_header.
* Macros for message handling
  INCLUDE mm_messages_mac.

  DATA: ls_mepoheader TYPE mepoheader,
        ls_pohead     TYPE  zme_pohead.

* Retrieve custom data
  ls_mepoheader = im_header->get_data( ).
  CALL FUNCTION 'Z_ME_CUST_DATA_GET'
    EXPORTING
      i_type  = 'HEADER'
      i_ebeln = ls_mepoheader-ebeln
    IMPORTING
      e_header = ls_pohead.

* Field ZK_FELD2 must contain the value 1 or 2
  IF ls_pohead-zk_feld2 NA '12'.
*    Following notifications refer to
*    metafield MMMFD_CUST_02:
     mmpur_metafield mmmfd_cust_02.
*    Display message:
*    "Value & is not a valid entry for field 2"
     mmpur_message_forced 'E' 'ZME' '001'
                          ls_pohead-zk_feld2 '' '' ''.
*    Purchase order must not be posted:
     im_header->invalidate( ).
```

```
        ENDIF.
ENDMETHOD.
```

Listing 3.24 Input Checks in PROCESS_HEAD

3.2 Customizing the Document Overview in Purchase Requisitions or Purchase Orders

This final part of the chapter introduces a still relatively unknown user exit, which you can use to customize the document overview in purchase requisitions or purchase orders (see Figure 3.7). It is also a simple matter of removing selection variants supplied in the SAP standard. You can also integrate custom queries into this view. For example, you can remove the existing PURCHASE ORDERS selection variant, and using a custom selection variant, replace this with a less-extensive selection screen. Two user exits are provided for this purpose, which can be found in the MEQUERY1 enhancement.

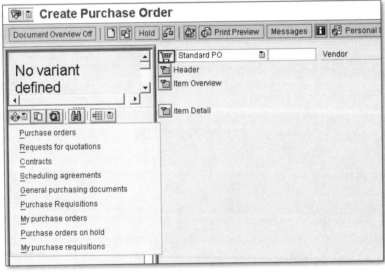

Figure 3.7 Selection Variants in the Document Overview

3.2.1 Removal of a Standard Selection Variant

The choice of selection variants is extensive. However, not every user requires this complete choice. For example, a user who only processes purchase requisitions but who doesn't have any authorization for purchase orders doesn't need the selection variants for queries, purchase orders, or contracts.

Cutting the existing choice is simple. Whenever the selection window is called (see Figure 3.7), the EXIT_SAPLMEQUERY_001 user exit is run. This user exit only has one internal table, META_TABLE, as a parameter (see Table 3.11), and each table line contains two fields: The first field CLASSID is an internal reference to the underlying selection; the second field LABEL contains the text as it is displayed in the document in the selection window.

CLASSID	LABEL
PO_QUERY	Purchase orders
RFQ_QUERY	Queries
AGREEMENT_QUERY	Contracts
SCH_QUERY	Scheduling agreements
PURDOCS_QUERY	General purchasing documents
REQ_QUERY	Purchase requisitions
POS_BY_USER_QUERY	My purchase orders
PARKED_POS_BY_USER_QUERY	Parked purchase orders
REQ_BY_USER_QUERY	My purchase order requisitions

Table 3.11   Standard Content of the Table META_TABLE

If you reduce this table simply by the nonrequired selection variants, then these are no longer displayed. To stay with the same example, you can implement an authorization check in this user exit that checks whether the user has the authorization to create purchase orders. If not, all entries, except the two for purchase requisitions (REQ_QUERY and REQ_BY_USER_QUERY), are deleted.

1. Create a new project and include the MEQUERY1 enhancement. The procedure for this is described in Section 2.1, Use of User Exits.

2. Navigate to the EXIT_SAPLMEQUERY_001 user exit, and then double-click on the ZXM02U10 include integrated there. Create the include if it doesn't yet exist.

3. An authorization check is now necessary. Because the MM authorization objects mostly check at the plant or purchasing organization level, the only subject of interest here is whether the user fundamentally has the authorization to create

the purchase order. The check for the transaction code can be used here. The respective authorization object is S_TCODE.

Click PATTERN, and select the option AUTHORITY CHECK in the dialog window that opens. Specify the object S_TCODE, and confirm the dialog window using the Enter key.

4. Replace the parameter behind the keyword FIELD with the transaction to be checked, that is, ME21N for the purchase order creation.

5. The AUTHORITY-CHECK command provides a sy-subrc unequal to 0 if the user doesn't hold the checked authorization. In this case, the undesired lines are now to be deleted. You can do this as usual via the DELETE command (see Listing 3.25).

```
*&---------------------------------------------------*
*&  Include           ZXM02U10
*&---------------------------------------------------*
*"*"Local interface:
*"  TABLES
*"      META_TABLE TYPE  MMPUR_DATABL_META_TABLE
*"---------------------------------------------------

* Authorization check on Transaction ME21N
AUTHORITY-CHECK OBJECT 'S_TCODE'
         ID 'TCD' FIELD 'ME21N'.

IF sy-subrc NE 0.
* No authorization for purchase order, remove all selection
* variants except REQ_QUERY and REQ_BY_USER_QUERY.
  DELETE meta_table WHERE classid NE 'REQ_QUERY' AND
                          classid NE 'REQ_BY_USER_QUERY'.
ENDIF.
```

Listing 3.25 Removing Selection Variants

6. Save and activate your coding.

7. Activate your project so that the user exit is active and will run. Test the result with a user who doesn't hold the respective authorization. You can view the result in Figure 3.8.

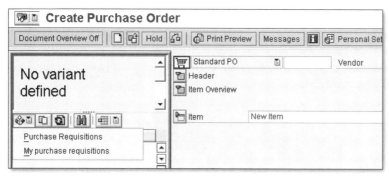

Figure 3.8 Reduced Document Overview with Only Two Selection Variants

3.2.2 Inserting Custom Selection Variants

The specified selection screen doesn't always suit your individual requirements. In the selection variant "Purchase Orders", for example, you can access nearly all fields via the dynamic selections. Perhaps you want to directly access fields from this selection in the initial screen.

You can create virtually every query by yourself and integrate it into the document overview. To do this, you need a report generated by SAP Query and the user exits EXIT_SAPLMEQUERY_001 and EXIT_SAPLMEQUERY_002.

Creating SAP Queries

The selection variants in the document overview have been implemented by SAP Query (Transaction SQ01). It's possible with SAP Query to display lists without any possessing knowledge about ABAP. To integrate a custom report, you must first create this in an SAP Query.

Concepts from the World of Queries

Several concepts are used in the environment of SAP Queries that may be somewhat confusing at first. The following explanations should help if you haven't had experience with SAP Queries:

▸ **Work area**
All objects for SAP Queries can either be created in the global or local area. The global area stands for objects independent of clients and the local area for the client-dependent objects. A mixture of objects from both areas isn't possible.

- ▶ **InfoSet**
  An InfoSet views a data source. The InfoSet specifies which database tables are provided, how they are linked with one another, and which fields can be used from these tables in subsequent queries. An InfoSet can be used for any number of queries. InfoSets are maintained in Transaction SQ02.

- ▶ **User group**
  Queries are bundled in a user group by logical association, for example, according to a working group or specialist department. InfoSets are assigned to user groups that are used by users to generate queries. A query is created in this case, but a user group is required.

- ▶ **Queries**
  The actual queries are generated in the Query Painter. Fields from an InfoSet can be assigned as selection fields or as output fields.

The first step is to create an InfoSet. However, there is a very comprehensive InfoSet already provided for purchase orders in the global work area: /SAPQUERY/MEPO. You can use the InfoSet /SAPQUERY/MEBANF for purchase requisitions.

1. Start Transaction SQ02, and make sure that you have chosen the global work area. If required, you can navigate to the global work area via the ENVIRONMENT • QUERY AREAS menu. Enter /SAPQUERY/MEPO as the name, and click on DISPLAY.

2. You can now view all of the tables and fields available on the left-hand side (see Figure 3.9). Get an initial overview, and exit the transaction again.

3. Start Transaction SQ01 (INFORMATION SYSTEMS • AD HOC REPORTS • SAP QUERY menu path). Switch the work area immediately if you haven't done this already in Step 1.

4. Because the query is only created for access from the purchase order and isn't supposed to be used by individual users directly in the SAP Query transactions, you need a custom user group. Go to ENVIRONMENT • USER GROUPS; enter the name of a custom group, for example, ZME_QUERY; and click CREATE. Enter an additional descriptive short text in the dialog window that opens, and click SAVE.

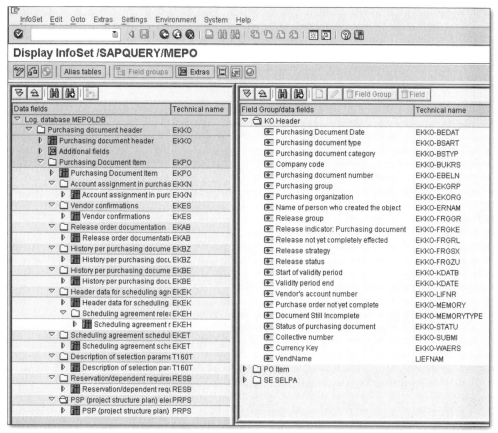

Figure 3.9 InfoSet /SAPQUERY/MEPO

5. Choose the Assign Users and InfoSets option. You can leave the list of assigned users blank. No user will work directly with this group. It is called later via the user exit. Choose instead the Assign InfoSets option in this dialog window. Scroll to the entry /SAPQUERY/MEPO, and checkmark this line. Click Save. Now go back three steps via Back (F3) until you are once again in the initial screen of SAP Query.

6. In the title bar, you can now see that the user group already generated has been directly selected. If this is not the group you want to use, you can change this via menu path Edit • OTHER USER GROUP.

7. Now create a query. You can choose, for example, the name ZME_BEST. Then click Create.

8. Select the InfoSet /SAPQUERY/MEPO by double-clicking in the dialog window that appears.

9. You now need to enter a title in the following screen. This title appears as a header when this selection is subsequently started. In the section OUTPUT FORMAT, activate the ABAP LIST option as well (see Figure 3.10).

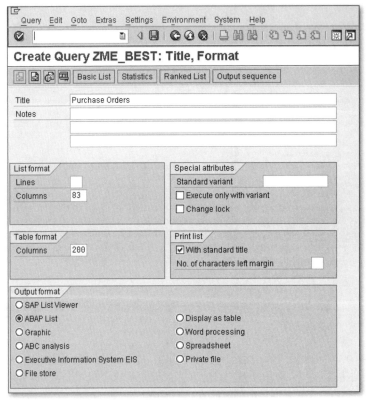

Figure 3.10 Creating an SAP Query

10. Check whether the graphical Query Painter is activated via the SETTINGS • SETTINGS menu. Finally, click on the BASIC LIST button.

11. Select the fields on the left-hand side that are supposed to appear as a selection field and a list box in the selection variant. For this example, you can mark the fields from Table 3.12, respectively.

Field Name	Description	List Box	Selection Field
EKKO-BEDAT	Date of the purchasing document	X	X
EKKO-BSTYP	Document type	X	
EKKO-EBELN	Document number	X	X
EKKO-EKGRP	Purchasing group		X
EKKO-ERNAM	Name of person responsible		X
EKKO-LIFNR	Vendor number	X	X
EKPO-EBELP	Item number	X	
EKPO-LOEKZ	Deletion indicator	X	X
EKPO-MATNR	Material number	X	X

Table 3.12 Field Selection for Query ZME_BEST

Note

If you want to use the selected documents via the ADOPT function of the document overview or by double-clicking the document number, you must include at least the following fields in a list box:

▶ **Purchase requisitions:** EBAN-BANFN (purchase requisition number) and EBAN-BNFPO (purchase requisition item).

▶ **Purchase orders:** EKKO-BSTYP (document type), EKKO-EBELN (document number), and EKPO-EBELP (document item).

12. Save your selection, and then exit Query Painter via BACK (F3).

13. You're now back in the initial screen of the ZME_BEST query (see Figure 3.10). Click TEST (Ctrl + F8) to execute the report. Leave the query for a variant empty in the dialog window that appears, and confirm the dialog window using the Enter key.

14. Change the entry MAX. NUMBER OF HITS to the value "250" in the GENERAL SELECTIONS area to avoid unnecessary comprehensive selections later. Then, click the disk icon to save a new variant. For example, enter ZME_BEST_STD as the name of the variant and a meaning (see Figure 3.11). Now hide all of the fields that aren't directly required for the query. These are all the fields below the DELETION INDICATOR field.

15. Now save the variant, and exit the query. You don't need to enter the variant as a standard variant. The assignment is made in the user exit.

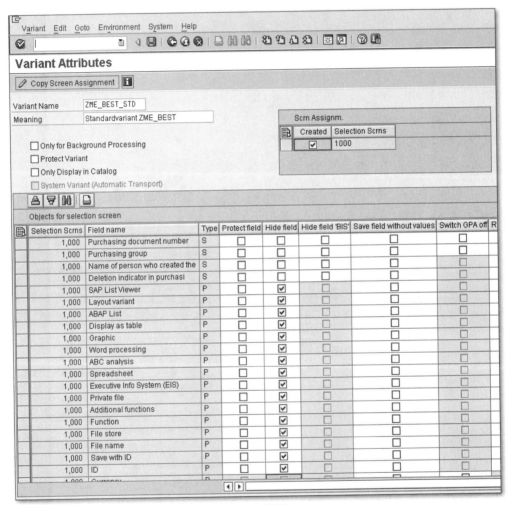

Figure 3.11 Variant Attributes for Query ZME_BEST

Providing the Selection Variant in the Document Overview

After you've successfully created the new query, you must still integrate it into the document overview. This happens via both user exits EXIT_SAPLMEQUERY_001 and EXIT_SAPLMEQUERY_002.

▶ To integrate a custom query in EXIT_SAPLMEQUERY_001, you first need to enhance the META_TABLE table (see Table 3.11) with a custom entry. The field CLASSID is used to identify the query later. You should begin the name with Z* to avoid overlaps. You can also choose the name freely. The LABEL field contains the title of the selection option as it should appear in the document view.

▶ EXIT_SAPLMEQUERY_002 is run as soon as the user has made a selection. The IM_CLASSID field contains the respective ID from the META_TABLE table. Therefore, check which CLASSID has been chosen. You can then call the respective query depending on this. Set the parameters according to Table 3.13.

Parameter	Content
CH_QUERY_NAME	Name of the query that you previously defined in Transaction SQ01.
CH_USERGROUP	Name of the user group assigned to the query.
CH_VARIANT	Name of the variant via which the query is to be started.
CH_WORKSPACE	The global work area is used with the value 'X'; the local work area is used without value.
CH_HANDLE	So that the drag-and-drop function for the shopping cart works, the system needs to know which type of document is returned. This is indicated by the handle: ▶ 0001: Purchase orders ▶ 0002: Purchase requisitions

Table 3.13 Parameters for Calling a Query

1. Edit the ZXM02U10 include from EXIT_SAPLMEQUERY_001. Add a custom entry to the META_TABLE table. You can find the complete coding of the exit following this change in Listing 3.26.

```
*&---------------------------------------------------------------*
*&  Include          ZXM02U10
*&---------------------------------------------------------------*
*"*"Local interface:
*"  TABLES
*"      META_TABLE TYPE  MMPUR_DATABL_META_TABLE
*"---------------------------------------------------------------
DATA: ls_meta_table LIKE LINE OF meta_table.

AUTHORITY-CHECK OBJECT 'S_TCODE'
```

```
            ID 'TCD' FIELD 'ME21N'.

IF sy-subrc NE 0.
* No authorization for purchase order, remove all
* selection variants except REQ_QUERY and REQ_BY_USER_QUERY
  delete meta_table where classid ne 'REQ_QUERY' AND
                          classid ne 'REQ_BY_USER_QUERY'.
ELSE.
* Insert new variant
  ls_meta_table-classid = 'Z_NEW_VAR'.
  ls_meta_table-label   = 'Bestellungen Neu'.
  append ls_meta_table to meta_table.
ENDIF.
```

Listing 3.26 Adding New Selection Variants

2. Now that you've included the new selection variant in the selection list, you need to make sure that the associated query is also called when the user has chosen the entry. Navigate to the EXIT_SAPLMEQUERY_002 user exit, and double-click the ZXM02U11 include integrated there. Create the include if it doesn't yet exist.

3. If the IM_CLASSID parameter contains the ID Z_NEW_VAR, call your query by transferring all of the parameters according to Table 3.13. Listing 3.27 contains the coding corresponding to the sample data.

```
*&----------------------------------------------------------*
*&  Include           ZXM02U11
*&----------------------------------------------------------*
IF im_classid = 'Z_NEW_VAR'.
* Name of query
  ch_query_name = 'ZME_BEST'.
* Name of the user group
  ch_usergroup = 'ZME_QUERY'.
* Variant for selection screen
  ch_variant = 'ZME_BEST_STD'.
* Handle: 0001 purchase orders
*         0002 - Purchase requisitions
  ch_handle = '0001'.
* Global work area
  ch_workspace = 'X'.
ENDIF.
```

Listing 3.27 Calling the Query

4 User Exits and BAdIs in External Services Management

External Services Management is in its broadest sense an enhancement to the typical purchase order to order services, to be rendered in the form of services and to enter and accept services rendered in a service entry sheet. There are numerous enhancements in this area; however, most only offer limited scope and functionality and seldom require comprehensive descriptions. This chapter covers the more extensive enhancements using simple examples — particularly those that make it easier for the user to enter data.

4.1 Prepopulating Account Assignment for Service Lines

When service lines from assigned purchasing documents are entered, the standard version displays a dialog window to the user (see Figure 4.1) to enter an account assignment. If this account assignment only seldom or never changes for individual users, a prepopulation can be carried out via the user exit EXIT_SAPLMLSK_001 from the enhancement SRVESKN. If this account assignment is clearly specified, the dialog window is no longer shown. This can save you a lot of time with document entry.

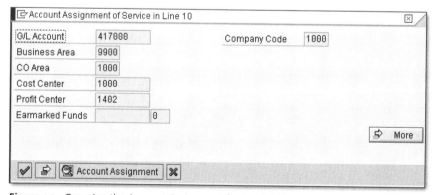

Figure 4.1 Querying the Account Assignment for Service Lines

In the following example, the user master should be read for the user entering the data. If the key "ABT20" has been maintained as the department there, the account assignment is specified according to fixed characteristics. Because this department mainly uses a free service entry that is assigned to the cost center, the cost center "1000" and the general ledger (GL) account "400000" are specified. The business area is also fixed and is therefore always included.

If the account assignment isn't complete, for example, because the user occasionally deviates from the normal procedure by choosing a project account assignment, causing the entry of a WBS element (work breakdown structure) to be necessary, the dialog window on the account assignment entry appears for the user to use.

You can now implement this example using the following step-by-step procedure:

1. Create a new project in Transaction CMOD. You can find details on this in Section 2.1.2, Creating a Project and Assigning Enhancements, in Chapter 2.

2. Switch to the user exit EXIT_SAPLMLSK_001, and generate the include ZXMLUU20 by double-clicking.

3. The user master is read first. This is possible via the function module BAPI_ USER_GET_DETAIL. You must only supply the parameter USERNAME with the current user (from the system field sy-uname). The department is located in the structure ADDRESS. Ignore all other return structures.

   As with many other BAPIs, this BAPI checks whether or not a specific return structure has been requested when called, and only then does it organize the necessary content. Therefore, if you only supply the parameters that you really need, the runtime of the BAPI is also reduced to a minimum.

4. If the department that is specified in the field ADDRESS-DEPARTMENT has the content "ABT20", the header structure T_ESKN is filled and appended to the internal table of the same name via the APPEND command. The most important fields of this structure are listed in Table 4.1, and the corresponding coding can be found in Listing 4.1.

Field	Description
WPROZ	Percentage of account assignment lines with regard to distribution in percentage terms
MENGE	Quantity reference of the current account assignment line with regard to distribution by quantity

Table 4.1 Important Fields of the Table T_ESKN (Excerpt)

Field	Description
SAKTO	GL account
GSBER	Business area
KOSTL	Cost center
AUFNR	Order number
PS_PSP_PNR	Work breakdown structure element (WBS element)
XBKST	Posting in cost center
XBAUF	Posting to order
XBPRO	Posting to project

Table 4.1 Important Fields of the Table T_ESKN (Excerpt) (Cont.)

```
*&-----------------------------------------------------------*
*&  Include          ZXMLUU20
*&-----------------------------------------------------------*
*"*"Local interface:
*"      IMPORTING
*"           VALUE(I_ESLL) LIKE  ESLL STRUCTURE  ESLL
*"      TABLES
*"           T_ESKN STRUCTURE  SRVESKN
*"-----------------------------------------------------------
DATA ls_address TYPE bapiaddr3.
DATA lt_return TYPE bapiret2_t.
DATA ls_return TYPE bapiret2.
DATA lv_subrc  TYPE sy-subrc.

* Retrieve access to user master, address data
CALL FUNCTION 'BAPI_USER_GET_DETAIL'
  EXPORTING
    username = sy-uname
  IMPORTING
    address  = ls_address
  TABLES
    return   = lt_return.

* Has an error occurred?
LOOP AT lt_return INTO ls_return.
  IF ls_return-type NA 'SIW'.
    lv_subrc = 4.
```

```
    EXIT.
  ENDIF.
ENDLOOP.

* Always prepopulate department ABT20
IF lv_subrc = 0 AND
   ls_address-department = 'ABT20'.
  t_eskn-wproz = 100.
  t_eskn-kostl = '1000'.
  t_eskn-sakto = '400000'.
  t_eskn-gsber = '9900'.
  APPEND t_eskn.

ENDIF.
```

Listing 4.1 Example for EXIT_SAPLMLSK_001

5. You also optionally have access to the service line itself (structure I_ESLL). You can influence the account assignment based on specific characteristics of the service line.

   The I_ESLL-VRTKZ field contains the distribution indicator, if a multiple account assignment is preset. You can define the settings for the account assignment screen in the Customizing for Purchasing under ACCOUNT ASSIGNMENT • MAINTAIN ACCOUNT ASSIGNMENT CATEGORIES. The account assignment screen (ID: ACCTASSGT SCRN) indicator must be set to 2 – MULTIPLE ACCOUNT ASSIGNMENT, and the DISTRIBUTION key must be set to a distribution type. If this indicator is set to 1 for distribution by quantity or to 2 for distribution in percentage terms, you can also add several lines to the internal Table T_ESKN to control the distribution. You set the distribution key via the field WPROZ or MENGE.

6. Don't forget to activate the project so that your user exit will actually run.

4.2   Input Check of the Service Lines

With the enhancement SRVESLL, you can carry out input checks when service lines are entered. There is also the alternative to prepopulate individual fields of a service line or overwrite these with a fixed value.

The enhancement SRVESLL consists of two user exits that are called at different times.

▶ EXIT_SAPLMLSP_030

This exit runs before the standard checks are carried out.

▶ EXIT_SAPLMLSP_031

This exit runs after all standard checks have been carried out.

Therefore, you'll normally use the EXIT_SAPLMLSP_031 for your input checks. However, you can also use the EXIT_SAPLMLSP_030 to prepopulate fields with specific values. All standard checks will still run after any possible changes.

4.2.1 Prepopulating Fields in EXIT_SAPLMLSP_030

The following brief example shows how you can prepopulate the fields of the service line from this exit. The USERF1_TXT user field populates the name of the person who created the service line. This field can be displayed again upon a subsequent acceptance, and therefore offers information to the person who entered the acceptance so that he doesn't need to look at the purchase order. This can facilitate contact when further questions arise.

1. Create a project again in Transaction CMOD. You can find details on this in Section 2.1.2, Creating a Project and Assigning Enhancements, in Chapter 2. Include the enhancement SRVESLL in your project.

2. Switch to the user exit EXIT_SAPLMLSP_030, and create the prepopulation of the field SRV_ESLL-USERF1_TXT. You must make sure that the exit will run only once for each service line in the screen, which also applies to empty lines in which the user hasn't made any entry. If you were to now overwrite the field in all lines, the user would receive an error message for these lines because the entry is incomplete.

   To avoid this, you need an additional check to determine whether this line is relevant at all. Here, you can use the field MENGE — the line will only be used when a quantity has been entered. A prepopulation will subsequently follow. A brief example is provided in Listing 4.2.

3. Don't forget to activate the project so that your enhancement will actually run.

```
*&---------------------------------------------------------------------*
*&  Include           ZXMLUU16
*&---------------------------------------------------------------------*
*"*"Local interface:
*"      CHANGING
```

```
*"              VALUE(SRV_ESLL) LIKE   ESLL STRUCTURE   ESLL
*"------------------------------------------------------------
* Prepopulating the fields of  the structure ESLL:
* Remember creator of the service line
IF srv_esll-menge > 0.
  srv_esll-userf1_txt = sy-uname.
ENDIF.
```

Listing 4.2 Example for EXIT_SAPLMLSP_030

4.2.2   Input Check in EXIT_SAPLMLSP_031

As already mentioned, you can use the exit EXIT_SAPLMLSP_031 by carrying out custom input checks because it will only run after the standard checks are implemented and the service line has its final status for the time being.

To show you an example, we must complete the field USERF2_TXT. Empty values aren't allowed.

1. Even here, you must first have a suitable project in Transaction CMOD to which you have assigned the enhancement SRVESLL.

2. Switch to the user exit EXIT_SAPLMLSP_031, and program your check. This exit actually only runs in contrast to EXIT_SAPLMLSP_030 when there is an entry made by the user. However, it doesn't do any harm to carry out an additional check on an existing quantity.

3. If the field USERF2_TXT isn't filled, an error message appears. So that the user is able to produce a reference, you should also include the number of the service line to this error message. This can be found in field SRV_ESLL-EXTROW. However, this field has been formatted so that the item number has been filled with leading zeros, which doesn't look nice when displayed on the screen. For this reason, you should copy the content into a custom field beforehand and then remove the leading zeros. Use the following command:

```
SHIFT <fieldname> LEFT DELETING LEADING '0'.
```

4. The service lines can be maintained from various purchasing documents and different transactions. Therefore, you can't use any message collector to display the error message as usual, for example, in the Enjoy purchase order (Transaction ME21N). Display the error message directly using the command MESSAGE. The brief example on this exit is given in Listing 4.3.

5. Don't forget to activate the project so that your enhancement will run.

```
*&----------------------------------------------------------*
*&  Include            ZXMLUU17
*&----------------------------------------------------------*
*"*"Local interface:
*"       IMPORTING
*"              VALUE(SRV_ESLL) LIKE  ESLL STRUCTURE  ESLL
*"----------------------------------------------------------
* Temporary field for display in message
DATA lv_extrow TYPE esll-extrow.

* Field USERF2_TXT must be filled:
IF srv_esll-userf2_txt IS INITIAL AND
   srv_esll-menge > 0.
* Message 100:
* 'Line &: Please complete user field 4'
   lv_extrow = srv_esll-extrow.
   SHIFT lv_extrow LEFT DELETING LEADING '0'.

   MESSAGE E100(ZSRV) WITH lv_extrow.
ENDIF.
```

Listing 4.3 Example for EXIT_SAPLMLSP_031

4.3 Prepopulation of the Header Data in the Data Entry Sheet

When you create a new data entry sheet (Transaction ML81N), some header data must first be filled out before the services can be entered or copied from the purchase order.

You can also set up prepopulations by using the user exit EXIT_SAPLMLSR_010, which is beneficial for the user. As an example, the short text on a new data entry sheet is supposed to be filled out automatically (see Figure 4.2).

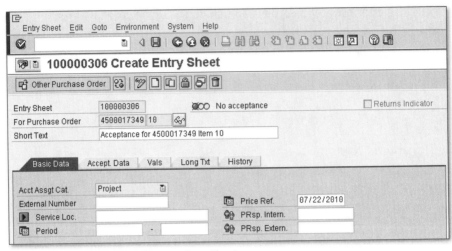

Figure 4.2 Header Data on the Data Entry Sheet

Proceed as follows:

1. Create a new project in Transaction CMOD, and include the enhancement SRVESSR.

2. Go directly to EXIT_SAPLMLSR_010, and enter the respective coding. All data for the purchase order is provided via the structures I_EKKO and I_EKPO. In the example given, the text "Acceptance of Purchase Order <Purchase Order Number> Item <Item>" is supposed to be created and used as a short text.

   The purchase order number is in the field I_EKKO-EBELN, and the item is in field I_EKPO-EBELP. You should remove the leading zeros again to display the item. If you use purchase orders with less than the usual 10 digits, you should also manage zeros for your purchase order number.

3. The example is given in Listing 4.4. Text literals have been used to create the short text. You can create these texts also as a text symbol (GoTo • TEXT ELEMENTS • TEXT SYMBOLS) and use these via the term TEXT-### instead of the literals in the coding. The advantage of this is that you can also use the texts via GoTo • TRANSLATION in other languages.

```
*&---------------------------------------------------*
*&  Include          ZXMLUU19
*&---------------------------------------------------*
*"*"Local interface:
*"       IMPORTING
```

```
*"              VALUE(I_EKKO) LIKE  EKKO STRUCTURE   EKKO
*"              VALUE(I_EKPO) LIKE  EKPO STRUCTURE   EKPO
*"       CHANGING
*"              VALUE(C_ESSR) LIKE  ESSR STRUCTURE   ESSR
*"------------------------------------------------------------
* Local fields for formatting
DATA lv_text  TYPE essr-txz01.
DATA lv_ebelp TYPE ekpo-ebelp.

IF c_essr-txz01 IS INITIAL.
* Remove leading zeros of the item
  lv_ebelp = i_ekpo-ebelp.
  SHIFT lv_ebelp LEFT DELETING LEADING '0'.
* Creating and assigning text
  CONCATENATE 'Abnahme zu'
              i_ekko-ebeln
              'Position'
              lv_ebelp
              INTO lv_text
              SEPARATED BY space.
  c_essr-txz01 = lv_text.
ENDIF.
```

Listing 4.4 Example for EXIT_SAPLMLSR_010

5 User Exits and BAdIs in Inventory Management

The concept of Inventory Management in SAP Materials Management (MM) basically involves summarizing the management of all warehouse stocks with regard to value and quantity as well as the associated goods movements. Because the conceivable processes in this core area are very comprehensive, there are also many setting options in the system. This is also reflected in the number of possible program-related enhancements. In this chapter, you will learn about the most important enhancements for Inventory Management.

5.1 Custom Fields in Transaction MIGO

With the implementation of the central Transaction MIGO for all goods movements, a powerful BAdI is provided: `MB_MIGO_BADI`. With this BAdI, you can integrate and post custom fields as custom tabstrips at the header and item level. You can also carry out input checks in your custom fields or populate many standard fields with default values.

> **Display of Custom Data**
>
> If you execute the following example, you may find that the subsequent display of the data of a posted material document at item level doesn't work. This is the case when SAP Note 1029951 has been manually imported into your system or support packages have been imported.
>
> As a result of the changes from this note, the method `LINE_MODIFY`, which is actually provided for reading the item data from the database, will no longer run when material documents are displayed. Unfortunately, it isn't possible to use another method for this because the associated standard item data (structure `GOITEM`) isn't provided in all other relevant methods, and you therefore cannot assign your data to a specific document line.
>
> With SAP Note 1477221, the method `LINE_MODIFY` will run again. If this note hasn't yet been released for customers when you read these lines, you can modify the program location relevant for the call of the method, as described in SAP Note 1136344. The example given here will be fully functional in both cases.

5.1.1 Custom Fields: An Overview

The capability of the BAdI MB_MIGO_BADI results in a certain amount of complexity. There are 17 methods that are called at many different times. Nevertheless, to make the next example as clear as possible, you'll only view the implementation of custom fields at the header and item level (see Figure 5.1). This reduces the BAdI to 11 methods with which the minimum requirements can be fulfilled. In a second step, you'll then learn about the function of the remaining methods in a brief overview.

Figure 5.1 Custom Fields in Transaction MIGO

Function Group for the Management of Dynpros

Just as with the custom fields in the purchase order (see Section 3.1, Custom Fields in Purchase Orders, in Chapter 3), you first need a function group to include the dynpros and some function modules for the exchange of data and for updating custom fields. However, this function group can be implemented for the BAdI MB_MIGO_BADI much more easily and must assume fewer tasks.

You have to work with two BAdIs in the purchase order to activate the custom fields. The function group therefore not only has to assume the communication with the dynpros but also must map the communication between the BAdIs. You can, however, execute all the necessary steps directly in the BAdI MB_MIGO_BADI for

Transaction MIGO, so additional communication with another BAdI isn't needed. You can create a dynpro in the function group for the header and item data and create two function modules for each dynpro to store and retrieve the data in the dynpro. You also need an update module to save your custom data. To post your custom data, you need to define custom tables in the ABAP Dictionary.

Usage of the BAdI MB_MIGO_BADI

As soon as you've created the function group, you can begin with the implementation of the BAdI. You keep the data on the custom fields for runtime in the attributes of the BAdI. First, these areas need to be defined.

MB_MIGO_BADI can be implemented many times. However, there are only five custom tabstrips for the header and item levels. For this reason, precisely five active implementations are allowed. The method INIT is activated when Transaction MIGO is started, and it's used to register an implementation and populate a tabstrip.

With the initialization of a document (new document or display of an existing document), the methods will run from Table 5.1. The methods MODE_SET and STATUS_AND_HEADER are also triggered when the document status changes.

Method	Description
RESET	This method is used to initialize all custom data in the attributes of the BAdI implementation.
MODE_SET	In this method, you obtain information on the action (goods receipt, goods issue, etc.) and the chosen reference (purchase order, reservation, etc.) chosen by the user; these are the fields that are always available in Transaction MIGO in the top-left side. You can evaluate this information, and store it in the attributes of the implementation for subsequent use.
STATUS_AND_HEADER	This method is mainly used to fill the custom header data when an existing document is read.

Table 5.1 Initialization of a Document and Status Change

The methods are also executed with each dialog step for header data from Table 5.2 and with each dialog step on item data from Table 5.3. The method LINE_MODIFY is also executed when a line is added either when the user makes an entry or when an existing material document is read from the database.

Method	Description
PBO_HEADER	This method is called before the header data are displayed. You must transfer the data to be displayed to the function group and specify the dynpro to be displayed. The tabstrip header is also specified here.
PAI_HEADER	This method runs as soon as the user has entered the data. You need to retrieve the possibly changed data from the function group.

Table 5.2 Methods in the Dialog Step on Header Data

Method	Description
PBO_DETAIL	This method is called before the item data is displayed. In the parameter I_LINE_ID, you obtain the current item and must transfer the associated data in the function group. You also need to specify the dynpro to be displayed as well as the header of the tabstrip here.
PAI_DETAIL	You retrieve the data from the dynpro after the user has entered it. First, check whether data has changed, and if applicable, set the parameter E_FORCE_CHANGE. The method LINE_MODIFY is activated when the parameter has been set.
LINE_MODIFY	This method is activated when a line has been changed (see PAI_DETAIL) or when a new line has been inserted. When adding new lines, you must initialize your custom fields, or if the document is being read in the display mode, you must read the data from the database. If required, you have the option here of writing standard fields that you've also possibly integrated in your dynpro back to the standard items.
LINE_DELETE	This method runs when the user has deleted a line of the material document. In this case, you also need to delete the associated custom data.

Table 5.3 Methods in the Dialog Step for Item Data

Finally, you must use the method POST_DOCUMENT to format your custom data and call the update module from your function group. The final line number for each document line is set only in this method, as contained in Table MSEG — that is, in the table in which the standard item data is stored. You should convert your custom data accordingly so that you can assign it more easily later on.

5.1.2 Preparations in the ABAP Dictionary

At this point, it makes sense to refer again to the general data definitions in the ABAP Dictionary. Both header and item data are implemented in this example, and two suitable database tables are required to store the data. The following example again only uses a simple variant for this, and only one text field is used as a custom field.

1. Switch to the ABAP Dictionary (Transaction SE11), and create the table for the header data. Besides the actual text field ZK_FELD1, you also need the key fields; that is, the material document number and posting year. The table name ZMB_MIGOHEAD has been used in the example. You can view the associated fields in Table 5.4.

Field Name	Key Field	Data Element
MANDT	Yes	MANDT
MBLNR	Yes	MBLNR
MJAHR	Yes	MJAHR
ZK_FELD1		CHAR32

Table 5.4 Fields of the Table ZMB_MIGOHEAD

2. Create the table for the item data. A line number is necessary besides the previously used key fields. The custom field is called ZP_FELD1 here. The table name ZMB_MIGOITEM is used. The associated fields can be viewed in Table 5.5.

Field Name	Key Field	Data Element
MANDT	Yes	MANDT
MBLNR	Yes	MBLNR
MJAHR	Yes	MJAHR
ZEILE	Yes	MBLPO
ZP_FELD1		CHAR32

Table 5.5 Fields of the Table ZMB_MIGOITEM

5.1.3   Preparation of the Function Group

You next need to deal with the function group and the dynpro. In this example, both the header and the item data are implemented. A dynpro is also required here. Moreover, two function modules for the data communication and one update module are necessary in each case. Another module informs the function group on the current status of Transaction MIGO. If this isn't in the display mode, the fields in the dynpros aren't ready for input.

1. Switch to Transaction SE80. Select the FUNCTION GROUP option in the Repository Browser, and specify ZMB_MIGO as the name. Press Enter. Confirm in the dialog that this function group should now be generated.

Dynpro Variations

In this example, a dynpro is defined for the header and item data in each case. You certainly have the option, however, of preparing different situations as well as different dynpros. Your requirement can, for example, be different in goods receipt than in goods issue. You decide which dynpro is actually displayed at runtime via your programming.

In the method MODE_SET of the BAdI MB_MIGO_BADI, you learn which action (displays, goods receipt, goods issue, etc.) has just been selected. You can keep this information in an attribute of the class and then dynamically set the dynpro in method PBO_HEADER or PBO_DETAIL based on this information.

---

2. Create the dynpro for the header data. Now right-click ZMB_MIGO in the object browser, and select CREATE • DYNPRO from the context menu. The dynpro number should be 0100. In the properties, you must set SUBSCREEN as the DYNPRO TYPE because other types cannot be integrated with tabstrips, and you would get a short dump upon implementation.

3. Click the LAYOUT button to switch to the Screen Painter. Here you choose DICTIONARY/PROGRAM FIELDS in the GOTO • SECONDARY WINDOW menu, or press F6. In the window displayed, specify ZMB_MIGOHEAD as the table name and press Enter. Mark the field ZK_FELD1, and press Enter again (see Figure 5.2). Using the mouse, now position the field in the top-left corner of the dynpro. Save and activate the dynpro, and then exit the Screen Painter.

4. Create the dynpro 0200 for the item data. Choose the field ZP_FELD1 from Table ZMB_MIGOITEM, and then proceed as in the previous step.

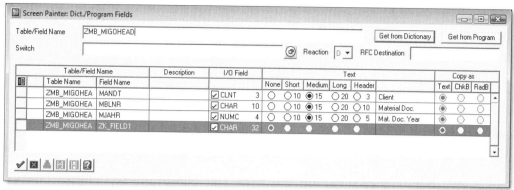

Figure 5.2 Dict/Program Fields Window

5. So that you are able to subsequently fill the fields in these dynpros with data, fields with an identical name must be available in the global data. Create these with the keyword TABLES. Furthermore, the fields are then ready for input only if the document isn't in a display mode. The mode is to be subsequently set via a function module. You can create it now, however, as a flag (gv_outputonly, data type C) in the global data.

You switch to the global data via the Object Browser by navigating to the include LZMB_MIGOTOP in the INCLUDES section. An example is given in Listing 5.1.

```
FUNCTION-POOL ZMB_MIGO.                    "MESSAGE-ID ..
* Work structures for dynpros
TABLES: zmb_migohead,
        zmb_migoitem.


* Display mode?
DATA gv_outputonly TYPE c.
```
Listing 5.1 Global Data in LZMB_MIGOTOP

6. If the flag gv_outputonly is set, then the fields in the dynpro aren't ready for input. Therefore, change to the flow logic of dynpro 0100. Remove the comments in the PROCESS BEFORE OUTPUT time from the STATUS_0100 module. Double-click the module name. To generate the module, use the suggested include name.

Set the value of SCREEN-INPUT based on the field gv_outputonly with a LOOP AT SCREEN. An example is given in Listing 5.2.

```
*------------------------------------------------------------*
***INCLUDE LZMB_MIGO001 .
*------------------------------------------------------------*
MODULE status_0100 OUTPUT.
  LOOP AT SCREEN.
    IF gv_outputonly IS INITIAL.
      screen-input = 1.
    ELSE.
      screen-input = 0.
    ENDIF.

    MODIFY SCREEN.
  ENDLOOP.
ENDMODULE.                      " STATUS_0100   OUTPUT
```
Listing 5.2 Flow Logic on Dynpro 0100

7. Dynpro 0200 is also not ready for input in the display mode. Switch to dynpro 0200, and proceed as in the previous step.

Next you can begin with the function modules:

1. An overview of the required modules is given in Table 5.6. Begin with the module ZMB_MIGO_SETSTATUS. You only need a flag as an input parameter; from this, you overwrite the global field gv_outputonly (see Listing 5.3).

Function Module	Description
ZMB_MIGO_SETSTATUS	Sets the flag gv_outputonly
ZMB_MIGO_HEAD_SET	Sets data for dynpro 100
ZMB_MIGO_HEAD_GET	Returns data from dynpro 100
ZMB_MIGO_ITEM_SET	Sets data for dynpro 200
ZMB_MIGO_ITEM_GET	Returns data from dynpro 200
ZMB_MIGO_POST	Updates header and item data

Table 5.6 Function Modules for Data Exchange

```
FUNCTION ZMB_MIGO_SETSTATUS.
*"------------------------------------------------------------
*"*"Local interface:
*"  IMPORTING
*"     REFERENCE(I_OUTPUTONLY) TYPE   C
```

```
*"------------------------------------------------------------
* Set input status
  gv_outputonly = i_outputonly.

ENDFUNCTION.
```

Listing 5.3 Coding on ZMB_MIGO_SETSTATUS

2. Create the modules ZMB_MIGO_HEAD_SET and ZMB_MIGO_HEAD_GET. You need a structure with Table ZMB_MIGOHEAD as a data type to use it as an import or export parameter. Simply copy the data in the respective direction between the parameters and the work structure previously defined with TABLES (see Listing 5.4 and Listing 5.5).

```
FUNCTION ZMB_MIGO_HEAD_SET.
*"------------------------------------------------------------
*"*"Local interface:
*"  IMPORTING
*"     REFERENCE(I_HEAD) TYPE  ZMB_MIGOHEAD
*"------------------------------------------------------------
* Prepare data for dynpro
  zmb_migohead = i_head.

ENDFUNCTION.
```

Listing 5.4 Coding on ZMB_MIGO_HEAD_SET

```
FUNCTION zmb_migo_head_get.
*"------------------------------------------------------------
*"*"Local interface:
*"  EXPORTING
*"     REFERENCE(E_HEAD) TYPE  ZMB_MIGOHEAD
*"------------------------------------------------------------
* Return data from dynpro
  e_head = zmb_migohead.

ENDFUNCTION.
```

Listing 5.5 Coding on ZMB_MIGO_HEAD_GET

3. For the function modules ZMB_MIGO_ITEM_SET and ZMB_MIGO_ITEM_GET, proceed exactly as before. Only use ZMB_MIGOITEM as a reference (see Listing 5.6 and Listing 5.7).

```
FUNCTION zmb_migo_item_set.
*"----------------------------------------------------------------
*"*"Local interface:
*"   IMPORTING
*"      REFERENCE(I_ITEM) TYPE  ZMB_MIGOITEM
*"----------------------------------------------------------------
* Prepare data for dynpro
  zmb_migoitem = i_item.

ENDFUNCTION.
```

Listing 5.6 Coding on ZMB_MIGO_ITEM_SET

```
FUNCTION ZMB_MIGO_ITEM_GET.
*"----------------------------------------------------------------
*"*"Local interface:
*"   EXPORTING
*"      REFERENCE(E_ITEM) TYPE  ZMB_MIGOITEM
*"----------------------------------------------------------------
* Return data from dynpro
  e_item = zmb_migoitem.

ENDFUNCTION.
```

Listing 5.7 Coding on ZMB_MIGO_ITEM_GET

4. Create the function module ZMB_MIGO_POST. The module must be marked in the PROCESSING TYPE section as an UPDATE MODULE (START IMMED.) (see Figure 5.3).

   Create an import parameter (suggestion I_HEAD) as a structure for Table ZMB_MIGOHEAD. Activate the PASS VALUE option for this parameter because no reference parameters are allowed in update modules. Then define a table parameter (suggestion T_ITEMS) with reference to Table ZMB_MIGOITEM.

5. With regard to update modules, you should always integrate several logical tests to prevent erroneous updates as much as possible. You need to check whether all key fields of the header and item data are filled. Otherwise, an exception will be triggered. To do this, create the DATA_ERROR exception in the EXCEPTIONS tabstrip.

   If the writing of the data fails, however, an exception will also be triggered. You create this exception as INSERT_ERROR. Triggering an exception results in an update termination, and if there's an error, the complete material document is not posted.

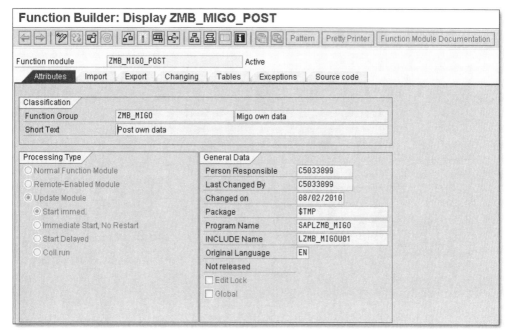

Figure 5.3 Properties of the Update Module

6. Switch to the SOURCE TEXT, and begin with the programming. Check whether the key fields of the header data are filled (parameter I_HEAD, fields MBLNR and MJAHR). Proceed exactly as before in a loop via the item data (Table T_ITEMS). Check also the line number (field ZEILE). If an error occurs, trigger the exception DATA_ERROR by using the command RAISE.

7. If no error occurs, update the data using the command INSERT. If an error occurs here (SY-SUBRC <> 0), trigger the exception INSERT_ERROR (see Listing 5.8).

```
FUNCTION zmb_migo_post.
*"----------------------------------------------------------
*"*"Update module:
*"
*"*"Local interface:
*"   IMPORTING
*"      VALUE(I_HEAD) TYPE  ZMB_MIGOHEAD
*"   TABLES
```

```
*"          T_ITEMS STRUCTURE  ZMB_MIGOITEM
*"  EXCEPTIONS
*"          INSERT_ERROR
*"          DATA_ERROR
*"------------------------------------------------------------

* Check transferred data
  IF i_head-mblnr IS INITIAL OR
     i_head-mjahr IS INITIAL.
    RAISE data_error.
  ENDIF.

  LOOP AT t_items.
    IF t_items-mblnr IS INITIAL OR
       t_items-mjahr IS INITIAL OR
       t_items-zeile IS INITIAL.
      RAISE data_error.
    ENDIF.
  ENDLOOP.

 * Write header data
   INSERT zmb_migohead FROM i_head.
   IF sy-subrc <> 0.
     RAISE insert_error.
   ENDIF.

 * Write item data
   INSERT zmb_migoitem FROM TABLE t_items.
   IF sy-subrc <> 0.
     RAISE insert_error.
   ENDIF.
ENDFUNCTION.
```

Listing 5.8 Coding on ZMB_MIGO_POST

8. Save all changes, and check whether all components of the function group have been activated.

5.1.4   Preparation and Status Management in MB_MIGO_BADI

From now on, you can completely focus on the BAdI. All preparations have been made. As described earlier, all necessary data are kept in the attributes of the class. These are therefore created first.

1. Switch to Transaction SE19, and create a new implementation for the BAdI MB_MIGO_BADI. Double-click the name of the implementing class ZCL_IM_MB_MIGO_BADI, and then switch to the ATTRIBUTES tabstrip.

2. Create the attributes according to Table 5.7. Consider the following notes:

   ▶ GC_CLASS
   Each implementation of the BAdI MB_MIGO_BADI must clearly be identified toward Transaction MIGO. This happens via a constant of the type MIGO_CLASS_ID, which you must define in the attributes because you use these in several areas. In the example given, the constant has been specified with the initial value 'MIGO_OWN'. Note that the single quotation marks are necessary here.

   ▶ GV_LINEID
   In this line number, always note the item transferred last in the dynpro.

   ▶ GV_ACTION
   This attribute contains the currently chosen action (see Table 5.8).

   ▶ GV_REFDOC
   This attribute contains the currently chosen reference document type (see Table 5.9).

   ▶ GS_HEADER
   This structure contains the current header data on your tabstrip.

   ▶ GT_ITEM
   This internal table contains all items on the current document. You can only define internal tables in the attributes when you refer to a table type defined in the ABAP Dictionary or you create a local type. In the following example, a local type (TT_MIGOITEM) has been used that is still currently unknown.

Attribute	Type	Visibility	Reference Type
GC_CLASS	Constant	Private	MIGO_CLASS_ID
GV_LINEID	Instance Attribute	Private	GOITEM-GLOBAL_COUNTER
GV_ACTION	Instance Attribute	Private	GOACTION
GV_REFDOC	Instance Attribute	Private	REFDOC
GS_HEADER	Instance Attribute	Private	ZMB_MIGOHEAD
GT_ITEM	Instance Attribute	Private	TT_MIGOITEM

Table 5.7 Attributes of the Implementing Class

Action/Operation	Description
A01	Goods receipt
A02	Return delivery
A03	Cancellation
A04	Display
A05	Release Goods receipt (GR) blocked stock
A06	Subsequent delivery
A07	Goods issue
A08	Transfer posting
A09	Remove from storage
A10	Place in storage
A11	Subsequent adjustment

Table 5.8 List of Actions in Transaction MIGO

Reference Document	Description
R01	Purchase order
R02	Material document
R03	Delivery note
R04	Inbound delivery
R05	Outbound delivery
R06	Transport
R07	Transport ID code
R08	Order
R09	Reservation
R10	Other

Table 5.9 List of the Possible Reference Documents in Transaction MIGO

3. Switch to the TYPES tabstrip to create the data type `TT_MIGOITEM`. To define a table, you need the direct type input (see Figure 5.4).

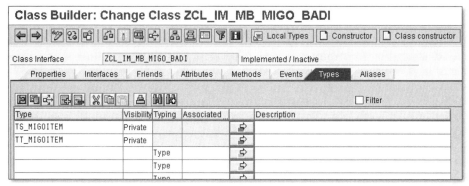

Figure 5.4 Enhanced Type Definition in Classes

4. Enter the name of the data type: `TT_MIGOITEM`.

5. Choose the PRIVATE entry in the VISIBILITY column because this type is only used within the class.

6. Click the yellow arrow icon on the right next to the reference type (direct type input). You're now in the ABAP Editor and can define the type as required.

7. Besides the actual data from table `ZMB_MIGOITEM`, the internal table requires another field `LINE_ID` that displays the internal number during the entry. Create a type that is made up of the field `LINE_ID` (type `MB_LINE_ID`) and `ZMB_MIGOITEM`. Name this type `TS_MIGOITEM`.

8. Define the type `TT_MIGOITEM` as an internal table for `TS_MIGOITEM`. The complete section should appear as follows:

```
PRIVATE SECTION.
   TYPES BEGIN OF ts_migoitem.
    TYPES line_id TYPE  mb_line_id.
    INCLUDE TYPE zmb_migoitem.
   TYPES END OF ts_migoitem.

   TYPES tt_migoitem TYPE TABLE OF ts_migoitem.
```

9. Save and activate your changes.

The first methods can now be programmed. Start with the method `INIT`. As described earlier, this method is used to announce the implementation in Transaction MIGO. A maximum of five implementations may be active at the same time.

You can now prepare the methods RESET and MODE_SET (refer to Table 5.1). You'll focus on the method STATUS_AND_HEADER later.

1. Switch to the METHODS tabstrip of the class ZCL_IM_MB_MIGO_BADI, and then navigate to method INIT. Here you must only transfer defined constants GC_CLASS to the internal Table CT_INIT in the attributes. This table may already contain other implementations. Therefore, don't overwrite the table; instead, attach your constant via APPEND. Because Table CT_INIT only consists of one field, you can attach the constant directly. You don't need a local structure (see Listing 5.9).

```
METHOD if_ex_mb_migo_badi~init.
* Register implementation
  APPEND gc_class TO ct_init.
ENDMETHOD.
```

Listing 5.9 Coding on the Method INIT

2. Edit the method RESET. This method is called when a new document is entered or loaded. Initialize the instance attributes of your class (see Listing 5.10).

```
METHOD if_ex_mb_migo_badi~reset.
* Initialize instance attributes
  CLEAR:  gv_lineid,
          gv_action,
          gv_refdoc,
          gs_header.
  REFRESH gt_item.
ENDMETHOD.
```

Listing 5.10 Coding on the Method RESET

3. Switch to the method MODE_SET. In this method, you obtain the chosen action (parameter I_ACTION; refer to Table 5.8) and the chosen reference document type (parameter I_REFDOC; refer to Table 5.9).

Your custom fields are only integrated when this allows the current action. You've already prepared the function module ZMB_MIGO_SETSTATUS, which you now call. Set the parameter I_OUTPUTONLY when the action A04 (Display) or A03 (Cancellation) is selected. Also note the current action in the attribute GV_ACTION and the reference document type in the attribute GV_REFDOC to be used later (see Listing 5.11).

```
METHOD if_ex_mb_migo_badi~mode_set.
* Local data declarations
  DATA lv_outputonly TYPE c.

* No input for action A04 or A03
  IF    i_action = 'A04' " Anzeige
     OR i_action = 'A03'. "Storno
    lv_outputonly = 'X'.
  ENDIF.

* Set current status
  CALL FUNCTION 'ZMB_MIGO_SETSTATUS'
    EXPORTING
      i_outputonly = lv_outputonly.

* Hold action
  gv_action = i_action.
* Hold reference document type
  gv_refdoc = i_refdoc.

ENDMETHOD.
```
Listing 5.11 Coding on the Method MODE_SET

5.1.5 Activation of Custom Header Data

Now let's move on to the relatively simple header data. At this point, your dynpro is displayed as a tabstrip, and data is exchanged between the BAdI and your dynpro. The reading of custom data is already implemented here when a posted document is open. You post the header data later, together with the item data.

1. Switch to the method PBO_HEADER. Start with a mandatory check: For technical reasons, the methods from all implementations are always called in an undefined sequence when one BAdI method is called to a method with several active implementations. At the same time, the method PBO_HEADER is called once for each of the five possible tabstrips. All implemented methods are therefore started each time. For this reason, you're informed of the class ID in the input parameter I_CLASS_ID (you've registered this in the method INIT; see Figure 5.5) that is associated with this call. You must make sure that you check whether the content of I_CLASS_ID corresponds to the class ID used in this implementation from constant GC_CLASS. Otherwise, unforeseeable side effects may arise.

2. The dynpro is registered next by transferring E_CPROG to the parameters and E_DYNNR to the program name and the dynpro number. In the parameter E_HEADING, specify the name of the tabstrip. In the example given, the dynpro 0100 is used in the program SAPLZMB_MIGO.

As an example, the tabstrip is only displayed when the operation refers to a purchase order document. You can check via the attribute GV_REFDOC whether you have filled this in method MODE_SET. The reference key for purchase orders is R01 (refer to Table 5.9).

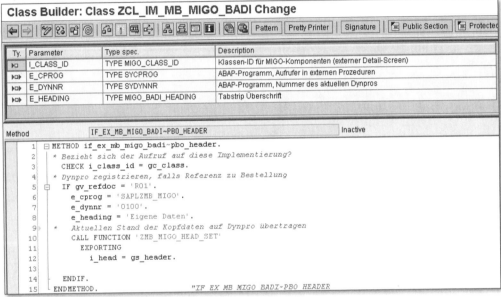

Figure 5.5 Interface of the Method PBO_HEADER

3. Finally, you still need to call the function module ZMB_MIGO_HEAD_SET and transfer the current content of the header data to the dynpro. The current status can always be found in the attribute GS_HEADER (see Listing 5.12).

```
METHOD if_ex_mb_migo_badi~pbo_header.
* Does the call refer to this implmentation?
  CHECK i_class_id = gc_class.

* Register dynpro if reference to purchase order
  IF gv_refdoc = 'R01'.
    e_cprog   = 'SAPLZMB_MIGO'.
```

```
      e_dynnr  = '0100'.
      e_heading = 'Eigene Daten'.

*    Transfer current status of the header data to dynpro
     CALL FUNCTION 'ZMB_MIGO_HEAD_SET'
       EXPORTING
         i_head = gs_header.

  ENDIF.
ENDMETHOD.
```

Listing 5.12 Coding on the Method PBO_HEADER

4. Now process the method `PAI_HEADER`. You only need to write the data from the dynpro back to the attribute `GS_HEADER` at this point. You do this by calling the function module `ZMB_MIGO_HEAD_GET` (see Listing 5.13).

```
METHOD if_ex_mb_migo_badi~pai_header.
* Retrieve data from the dynpro
  CALL FUNCTION 'ZMB_MIGO_HEAD_GET'
    IMPORTING
      e_head = gs_header.

ENDMETHOD.
```

Listing 5.13 Coding on the Method PAI_HEADER

5. You must also read the custom data from the database if required, and transfer it to the attribute `GS_HEADER`. You carry this out in method `STATUS_AND_HEADER`. Rereading the data is only necessary when an already-posted document is displayed or canceled. Therefore, you can check the action (attribute `GV_ACTION`) again here.

You read the data from the table `ZMB_MIGOHEAD` by using key fields `MBLNR` (material document number) and `MJAHR` (posting year) that are available in the `IS_GOHEAD` parameter (see Listing 5.14).

```
METHOD if_ex_mb_migo_badi~status_and_header.
* If an already posted document is to be displayed
* or canceled, read custom fields
* also from database.

  IF  gv_action = 'A04'  " Anzeige
    OR gv_action = 'A03'. " Storno
```

```
*    Read data from database
     SELECT SINGLE *
        FROM ZMB_MIGOHEAD
        INTO gs_header
        WHERE mblnr = is_gohead-mblnr
        AND   mjahr = is_gohead-mjahr.
   ENDIF.
ENDMETHOD.
```

Listing 5.14 Coding on the Method STATUS_AND_HEADER

Note Data

You can also set the parameter E_HOLD_DATA_DISABLE as an option in the method STA-TUS_AND_HEADER to prohibit the function HOLD. If you continue to allow the noting of material documents, you should program the methods HOLD_DATA_SAVE, HOLD_DATA_LOAD, and HOLD_DATA_DELETE so that your custom data can also be noted. You can obtain further information on this in Section 5.2.1, Noting Custom Data.

5.1.6 Activation of Custom Item Data

The actual activation of the item tabstrip works in a similar way to that of the header tabstrip. The communication with the dynpro and the management of the item data is slightly more time-consuming. Ultimately, there are several items in a document that must always be correctly assigned.

1. Start with the method PBO_DETAIL to register the item tabstrip and prepare the data. It's also important to check the class ID just as you did before with the header data.

2. In the parameter I_LINE_ID, you can find the line number that is being processed. All subsequent actions are only carried out when the parameter has a content unequal to zero.

   You need to also note this line number in the attribute GV_LINEID so that you can check later which line is actually being displayed in the dynpro.

3. There are also three parameters here, E_CPROG, E_DYNNR, and E_HEADING, to specify the program name, the dynpro number, and the caption of the tabstrip. The item tabstrip always appears in the example regardless of the reference document type.

4. You must then read the current line according to parameter I_LINE_ID from your internal table defined in the attributes GT_ITEM and transfer it to your function group by calling the function module ZMB_MIGO_ITEM_SET. Make sure that you copy the data via MOVECORRESPONDING into a structure suitable for the function module because your table with additional line ID has been defined in the attributes (see Listing 5.15).

```
METHOD if_ex_mb_migo_badi~pbo_detail.
* Local declarations
  DATA ls_item TYPE ts_migoitem.
  DATA ls_dynpro TYPE zmb_migoitem.

* Does the call refer to this implementation?
  CHECK i_class_id = gc_class.

* Has a line been set?
  CHECK i_line_id <> 0.

* Hold line
  gv_lineid = i_line_id.

* Register dynpro
  e_cprog   = 'SAPLZMB_MIGO'.
  e_dynnr   = '0200'.
  e_heading = 'Eigene Daten'.

* Read line from internal table
  READ TABLE gt_item
       INTO ls_item
       WITH KEY line_id = i_line_id.

* Copy necessary fields
  MOVE-CORRESPONDING ls_item TO ls_dynpro.
* Prepare line in dynpro
  CALL FUNCTION ZMB_MIGO_ITEM_SET'
    EXPORTING
      i_item = ls_dynpro.

ENDMETHOD.
```

Listing 5.15 Coding on the Method PBO_DETAIL

5. Switch to the method `PAI_DETAIL` in which you retrieve your data from the dynpro, and check whether the content has changed. If it has, set the flag `E_FORCE_CHANGE` through which the method `LINE_MODIFY` is triggered. Then carry out the actual handling of the data. The advantage to this is that the complete item management can be found in one central position (see Listing 5.16).

```
METHOD if_ex_mb_migo_badi~pai_detail.
* Local declarations
  DATA: ls_olddata TYPE zmb_migoitem,
        ls_newdata TYPE zmb_migoitem,
        ls_item TYPE ts_migoitem.


* Has a line been set?
  CHECK i_line_id <> 0.

* Retrieve old status from internal table
  READ TABLE gt_item
       INTO ls_item
       WITH KEY line_id = i_line_id.
  MOVE-CORRESPONDING ls_item TO ls_olddata.

* Retrieve new status from dynpro
  CALL FUNCTION 'ZMB_MIGO_ITEM_GET'
    IMPORTING
      e_item = ls_newdata.

* Check whether the data has been changed
  IF ls_olddata <> ls_newdata.
*    Trigger execution of LINE_MODIFY
     e_force_change = 'X'.
  ENDIF.

ENDMETHOD.
```

Listing 5.16 Coding on the Method PAI_DETAIL

6. Now it's time for the method `LINE_MODIFY`. As mentioned earlier, in this method, you manage not only possible changes to existing lines but also the insertion of new document lines in one central position.

As a parameter, you obtain the number of the current line in `I_LINE_ID`. With this line number, you must first of all check which case is actually present. Read the table `GT_ITEM` using this key. If the line already exists, possible changes must be transferred. If this line is not yet contained in `GT_ITEM`, you need to initialize the line and add the table. If the document is currently being read, at this point also read your custom data from the database.

Take a look at the case of a change. To ensure that the line being handled in the BAdI is also the line that is currently in the dynpro, compare the parameter `I_LINE_ID` with the previously noted line in the attribute `GV_LINEID`. You carry out the following steps only when the comparison is successful:

1. Retrieve the data from the dynpro by calling the function module `ZMB_MIGO_ITEM_GET` again. Copy the data received into a work structure that fits Table `GT_ITEM` (data type `TS_MIGOITEM`), and enhance the line at the current `LINE_ID`. Then write the changes back to Table `GT_ITEM`.

2. If the line doesn't yet exist, you must first check whether it's a line that has already been posted. In this case, the fields `CS_GOITEM-MBLNR` (material document number), `CS_GOITEM-MJAHR` (posting year), and `CS_GOITEM-ZEILE` (document item) are filled. Read your data from Table `ZMB_MIGOITEM` using these fields as a key, and copy these again into a suitable work structure for Table `GT_ITEM`.

   If the line doesn't yet exist in the database, leave the work structure empty, apart from the line `LINE_ID`, which you still need to enhance in both cases. Then write the new line in Table `GT_ITEM` (see Listing 5.17).

```
METHOD if_ex_mb_migo_badi~line_modify.
* Local declarations
  DATA lv_tabix TYPE sy-tabix.
  DATA ls_item TYPE ts_migoitem.
  DATA ls_newdata TYPE zmb_migoitem.

* Does the line already exist?
  READ TABLE gt_item INTO ls_item
    WITH KEY line_id = i_line_id.
  lv_tabix = sy-tabix.

  IF sy-subrc = 0.
*    Line exists already, does change
*    correspond to line in the BAdI of the dynpro line?
    CHECK i_line_id = gv_lineid.
```

```
*    Retrieve data from dynpro
     CALL FUNCTION 'ZMB_MIGO_ITEM_GET'
       IMPORTING
         e_item = ls_newdata.

*    Format changes
     MOVE-CORRESPONDING ls_newdata TO ls_item.
     ls_item-line_id = i_line_id.

*    Write back in table gt_item
     MODIFY gt_item FROM ls_item INDEX lv_tabix.
   ELSE.
*    Line doesn't yet exist, insert
     IF cs_goitem-mblnr IS NOT INITIAL AND
        cs_goitem-mjahr IS NOT INITIAL AND
        cs_goitem-zeile IS NOT INITIAL.
*      Line refers to an existing
*      material document, retrieve data from database
       SELECT SINGLE * FROM zmb_migoitem
                       INTO ls_newdata
                       WHERE mblnr = cs_goitem-mblnr AND
                             mjahr = cs_goitem-mjahr AND
                             zeile = cs_goitem-zeile.
       IF sy-subrc = 0.
*        Copy data
         MOVE-CORRESPONDING ls_newdata TO ls_item.
       ENDIF.
     ENDIF.
*    Build line with line ID and copy
*    to internal table
     ls_item-line_id = i_line_id.
     APPEND ls_item TO gt_item.
   ENDIF.

ENDMETHOD.
```

Listing 5.17 Coding on the Method LINE_MODIFY

3. Now you need to program the method LINE_DELETE. The method is called when a document item is deleted. In this case, you must also delete the associated custom data from Table GT_ITEM. Parameter I_LINE_ID is provided for you to identify the suitable line (see Listing 5.18).

```
METHOD if_ex_mb_migo_badi~line_delete.
* Delete line
  DELETE gt_item WHERE line_id = i_line_id.
ENDMETHOD.
```

Listing 5.18 Coding on the Method LINE_DELETE

5.1.7   Updating the Data

Now that you've fully programmed the internal handling of the data, you must ensure that your data is also posted when the material document is updated. To accomplish this, the method POST_DOCUMENT runs while the data is being posted.

1. Switch to the method POST_DOCUMENT. Before you can call your update modules, you must prepare the data. The structure GS_HEADER, which has been defined in the attributes, must still be enhanced in the document number. You obtain this structure via the parameter IS_MKPF. You can copy the values via a simple MOVE-CORRESPONDING.

2. Regarding item data, so far you have managed the data via the LINE_ID, that is, the internal line number. As you know, only the items for which the user has selected the OK field in Transaction MIGO are updated while being posted. Therefore, the table to be updated, MSEG, which is transferred to you as the parameter IT_MSEG, can have a different line numbering. The item number here is specified via the field ZEILE, and you must now convert your data to this line number. However, because Table IT_MSEG also contains the original LINE_ID besides the line number, this isn't a problem.

   Simply process all your custom item data from the internal Table GT_ITEM in a loop, and read the associated line from Table IT_MSEG using the field LINE_ID. You can then fill a structure for Table ZMB_MIGOITEM from both data structures. From the structure for Table IT_MSEG, copy the key fields, and from the structure on GT_ITEM, copy the custom fields. Add the result of a local internal table that also uses the type ZMB_MIGOITEM.

3. You now only need to call the function module ZMB_MIGO_POST and transfer the formatted header data and item data. Don't forget the addition IN UPDATE TASK, so that the function module in the updating is called (see Listing 5.19).

```
METHOD if_ex_mb_migo_badi~post_document.
* Local data declarations
  DATA: ls_item TYPE ts_migoitem,
```

```
            ls_mseg TYPE mseg,
            ls_migoitem TYPE zmb_migoitem,
            lt_migoitem TYPE TABLE OF zmb_migoitem.

* Prepare header data
* The key fields (material document number, posting year)
* are copied from the standard data (IS_MKPF)
   MOVE-CORRESPONDING is_mkpf TO gs_header.

* Prepare item data
   LOOP AT gt_item INTO ls_item.
*    Determine corresponding line in IT_MSEG.
*    Conversion between  LINE_ID and ZEILE
*    LINE_ID: internal line ID during entry
*    ZEILE:   Line number in table MSEG
     READ TABLE it_mseg
          INTO ls_mseg
          WITH KEY line_id = ls_item-line_id.
     IF sy-subrc = 0.
       MOVE-CORRESPONDING ls_item TO ls_migoitem.
       MOVE-CORRESPONDING ls_mseg TO ls_migoitem.
       APPEND ls_migoitem TO lt_migoitem.
     ENDIF.
   ENDLOOP.

* Updating of the data
   CALL FUNCTION 'ZMB_MIGO_POST'
     IN UPDATE TASK
     EXPORTING
       i_head  = gs_header
     TABLES
       t_items = lt_migoitem.

ENDMETHOD.
```

Listing 5.19 Coding on the Method POST_DOCUMENT

5.2   Other Functions of the BAdI MB_MIGO_BADI

After you've implemented custom fields via the BAdI MB_MIGO_BADI in the previous chapter, you already know all the fundamentals on this BAdI. Using other methods, you can still implement additional functions, particularly to further extend the functionality behind your custom fields.

5.2.1 Noting Custom Data

If you haven't prohibited the function Note in the method STATUS_AND_HEADER (*see* Section 5.1.5, Activation of Custom Header Data), you should ensure that your custom fields are also noted. Because a noted document isn't actually posted yet, it still doesn't have any material document number under which it can be stored. The data are instead clearly identified by a 22-digit GUID (Global Unique Identifier). Standard data are stored under this key in Table MMIM_PRED.

Three methods are available for storing your custom data: HOLD_DATA_SAVE, HOLD_DATA_LOAD, and HOLD_DATA_DELETE. The GUID, which has also been used for the standard fields, will transfer each of these methods as input parameters. Whether you now store your data, that is, the header data that are in the structure GS_HEADER and the item data in internal Table GT_ITEM, is up to you.

You have several options for storing the data:

▶ You can copy Tables ZMB_MIGOHEAD and ZMB_MIGOITEM and provide them with a GUID field as the key field. This makes saving somewhat more time-consuming, however, and when you add another custom field later to the original tables, you must also implement such enhancements in the Hold function.

▶ One alternative allows the comfortable, dynamic storage of both objects without any additional customization effort. You have the option in ABAP to serialize complex variables such as structures or internal tables; that is, to convert them into a character string. This string must have a very special data type. Use the type XSTRINGin ABAP and type RAWSTRING in the ABAP Dictionary. You then convert the data via the command EXPORT ... TO DATA BUFFER. You can store the result of the conversion in a field of a database line, regardless of whether or not this object has displayed an internal table with many lines beforehand. If the data is subsequently retrieved, using the command IMPORT ... FROM DATA BUFFER performs a reconversion in the actual object.

Based on the example of custom fields in Section 5.1, Custom Fields in Transaction MIGO, the following example shows you how simply you can temporarily store your data:

1. Your header and item data must be stored in a custom table. The data is saved under a GUID, which you obtain in the methods. You also need a field of the type RAWSTRING for the header data and the item data.

   Navigate to the ABAP Dictionary (Transaction SE11), and create a new table. Name this table ZMB_MIGOHOLD, for example.

2. Maintain the fields according to Table 5.10. The data element ZMB_RAW doesn't yet exist. You can create this by double-clicking. Don't use any domains to generate the data element, but choose the INTEGRATED TYPE option in the DATA TYPE tabstrip, and enter RAWSTRING here. Activate your data element, and then navigate back to the table.

Field Name	Key Field	Data Element
MANDT	Yes	MANDT
GUID	Yes	GUID
HHEAD		ZMB_RAW (Definition: Integrated type RAWSTRING)
HITEMS		ZMB_RAW

Table 5.10 Structure of the Table ZMB_MIGOHOLD

3. Maintain the technical settings of the table, and then activate the table.

4. Switch to your BAdI implementation, and navigate to the method HOLD_DATA_ SAVE. Create a local structure for Table ZMB_MIGOHOLD, and fill the GUID field from the input parameter I_GUID.

5. Fill the fields HHEAD and HITEMS from your attributes S_HEADER and GT_ITEM via the command EXPORT, which has the following structure:

```
EXPORT <id> FROM <variable> TO DATA BUFFER
  <ziel> COMPRESSION ON.
```

   <id> is any ID, <variable> is the source object that is to be converted, and <target> is the target variable of the type RAWSTRING. The addition, COMPRES-SION ON, is optional and compresses the data. This saves space in the database. The subsequent IMPORT automatically recognizes whether the data has been compressed, and extracts the data accordingly.

6. Finally, save your local structure via INSERT in the database (see Listing 5.20).

```
METHOD if_ex_mb_migo_badi~hold_data_save.
* Local work structure for ZMB_MIGOHOLD
  DATA ls_migohold TYPE zmb_migohold.

* Copy GUID
  ls_migohold-guid = i_guid.

* Convert header data in RAWSTRING/XSTRING
  EXPORT header FROM gs_header TO DATA BUFFER
     ls_migohold-hhead COMPRESSION ON.

* Convert item data in RAWSTRING/XSTRING
  EXPORT item FROM gt_item TO DATA BUFFER
     ls_migohold-hitems  COMPRESSION ON.

* Store data in database
  INSERT into zmb_migohold values ls_migohold.

ENDMETHOD.
```
Listing 5.20 Coding on the Method HOLD_DATA_SAVE

Now focus on the method HOLD_DATA_LOAD, which is called when a held document is loaded back.

1. Here you must load back the data from Table ZMB_MIGOHOLD using the retransferred GUID, and fill the attributes GS_HEADER and GT_ITEM from this.

2. Create a new local work structure for Table ZB_MIGOHOLD, and read the data via SELECT using the key in parameter I_GUID from your table.

3. You perform the reconversion from the fields HHEAD and HITEMS via the IMPORT function with the following structure:

```
IMPORT <id> TO <variable> FROM DATA BUFFER <quelle>.
```

<id> stands for the ID that you've used with regard to the EXPORT; <variable> is the target variable in which the result is to be written, that is, GS_HEADER or GT_ITEM; and <source> is the RAWSTRING field from your work structure for ZMB_MIGOHOLD. You can find an example on this method in Listing 5.21.

```
METHOD if_ex_mb_migo_badi~hold_data_load.
* Local work structure for ZMB_MIGOHOLD
  DATA ls_migohold TYPE zmb_migohold.

* Read held data using I_GUID
```

```
SELECT SINGLE * FROM zmb_migohold
      INTO ls_migohold
      WHERE guid = i_guid.

 IF sy-subrc = 0.
*    Convert header data in original object
      IMPORT header TO gs_header FROM DATA BUFFER
        ls_migohold-hhead.

*    Convert item data in original object
      IMPORT item TO gt_item FROM DATA BUFFER
        ls_migohold-hitems.
   ENDIF.
ENDMETHOD.
```

Listing 5.21 Coding on the Method HOLD_DATA_LOAD

4. If you delete the marked data, you must also remove your noted data. To do this, the method HOLD_DATA_DELETE is used. You also get the GUID as an input parameter again. Simply delete the associated record in Table ZMB_MIGOHOLD (see Listing 5.22).

```
METHOD if_ex_mb_migo_badi~hold_data_delete.
* Delete held data
  DELETE FROM zmb_migohold WHERE guid = i_guid.
ENDMETHOD.
```

Listing 5.22 Coding on the Method HOLD_DATA_DELETE

Changes to the Data Structure

As you've seen, you can easily convert ABAP structures in a RAWSTRING using the commands EXPORT and IMPORT, and copy these back to a structure. However, what happens when you change such a packed structure later on?

For example, if you add another field to Table ZMB_MIGOHEAD for the header data, data could still exist in the HHEAD field of the ZMB_MIGOHOLD table, which does not contain this new field. However, this generally doesn't constitute any problem. The command IMPORT copies the suitable part back to the work structure while reading the noted data, and the new field simply remains empty.

Vice versa is a bit more difficult. If you delete the second field again at a later stage and still contain noted data in the RAWSTRING HHEAD of this, you obtain a short dump when you IMPORT. You can avoid this dump by using the ACCEPTING TRUNCATION addition:

IMPORT <id> TO <variable> FROM DATA BUFFER <source> ACCEPTING TRUNCATION.

For major structure changes, you should delete the content of Table ZMB_MIGOHOLD as soon as you transport your changes to the production system.

5.2.2 Input Checks in Transaction MIGO

Two more methods are provided for checking your custom data: CHECK_HEADER and CHECK_ITEM. These methods are only carried out when the user chooses the CHECK or POST function. Follow the example below to activate the checks.

You need to carry out the checks on the attributes of your class in both cases. To do this, you obtain the input parameter I_LINE_ID for the items. If a warning or error message is displayed, this isn't allowed to happen directly via the MESSAGE command. Instead, you need to fill a return-table. You might know about this from using the BAPI function modules. The name of this return-table is in both methods: ET_BAPIRET2. Your messages are therefore displayed in the standard error log (see Figure 5.6) of Transaction MIGO, and the item number for item-related messages, to which the message refers, is displayed by default.

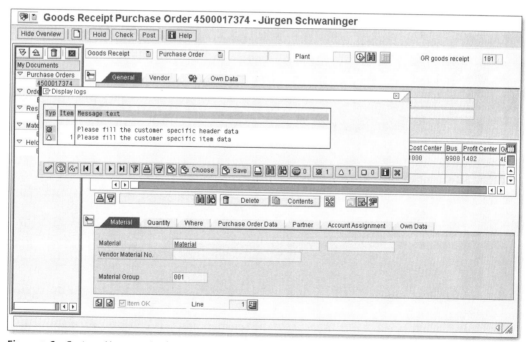

Figure 5.6 Custom Messages in the Error Log

1. Switch to the method CHECK_HEADER. For the return of messages, you must first define a work structure for the return-table by using the type BAPIRET2. This type is the line type that has been used to define internal Table ET_BAPIRET2. This type therefore contains the fields required for a message (see Table 5.11).

2. Now check whether the ZK_FELD1 field is filled from the attribute GS_HEADER. If this isn't the case, an error message appears.

3. To display the message, fill the fields of your work structure according to Table 5.11. Then copy the structure to internal Table ET_BAPIRET2, which is defined in the interface of the method (see Listing 5.23).

Field	Description
TYPE	Type of message, for example, 'E' for error messages or 'W' for warning messages
ID	Message class
NUMBER	Message number
MESSAGE_V1 – MESSAGE_V4	Optional message variables 1-4 that can be included

Table 5.11 Fields of the Return-Table

```
METHOD if_ex_mb_migo_badi~check_header.
* Local declaration on the return table
  DATA: ls_bapiret TYPE bapiret2.

* Header field must be filled!
  IF gs_header-zk_feld1 IS INITIAL.
*   Configure error message
    ls_bapiret-type       = 'E'.
    ls_bapiret-id         = 'ZMB'.
    ls_bapiret-number     = '050'.
    APPEND ls_bapiret TO et_bapiret2.
  ENDIF.

ENDMETHOD.
```

Listing 5.23 Coding on the Method CHECK_HEADER

4. Switch to the method CHECK_ITEM. You basically proceed here as you did with checking the header data. However, you must also define a local work structure

for your items, and read the suitable item from Table GT_ITEM using the input parameter I_LINE_ID.

5. You can then carry out your check again. The user should also fill the field ZP_FELD1. However, only a warning message is displayed if the field is empty (see Listing 5.24).

```
METHOD if_ex_mb_migo_badi~check_item.
* Local declarations
  DATA: ls_item TYPE ts_migoitem,
        ls_bapiret TYPE bapiret2.

* Read item from GT_ITEM
  READ TABLE gt_item INTO ls_item
       WITH KEY line_id = i_line_id.

  IF ls_item-zp_feld1 IS INITIAL.
*    Configure warning message
     ls_bapiret-type      = 'W'.
     ls_bapiret-id        = 'ZMB'.
     ls_bapiret-number    = '051'.
     APPEND ls_bapiret TO et_bapiret2.
  ENDIF.
ENDMETHOD.
```

Listing 5.24 Coding on the Method CHECK_ITEM

5.3   Checking and Prepopulating Standard Fields

Standard fields aren't provided in the check methods of the BAdI MB_MIGO_BADI. However, you can use the BAdI MB_MIGO_ITEM_BADI to also check these fields. Furthermore, in this BAdI, you can simply prepopulate the storage location or the item text. If other fields are prepopulated, you can take another look at the method LINE_MODIFY in the BAdI MB_MIGO_BADI, which provides more options in this context.

5.3.1   Prepopulation of Storage Location and Text

The only method of the BAdI MB_MIGO_ITEM_BADI, ITEM_MODIFY is called when new items are added or the user chooses the CHECK or POST function. When you fill the export parameter E_STGE_LOC (storage location) or E_ITEM_TEXT (item text) in the method, these values are set for all new additional items.

5.3.2 Checking the Standard Fields

If the user chooses the CHECK or POST functions, you can carry out custom checks and prevent posting if applicable. For this, the header data in parameter IS_GOHEAD and the item data table IS_GOITEM are provided.

If a message is displayed, you also need a work structure for a return-table with the type BAPIRET2. Fill the work structure according to Table 5.11 in Section 5.2.2, Input Checks in Transaction MIGO, and then append the message to internal Table ET_RETURN, which is also defined in the interface. Because the method ITEM_MODIFY could be called repeatedly, and Table ET_RETURN is already filled by the previous call, you should first delete the content; otherwise, the same message could possibly appear twice in the message log (see Listing 5.25).

```
METHOD if_ex_mb_migo_item_badi~item_modify.
* Local work structure for the return- table
  DATA: ls_bapiret TYPE bapiret2.

* For plant 1000 storage location 0001 is always
* to be suggested.
  IF is_goitem-werks = '1000'.
    e_stge_loc = '0001'.
  ENDIF.

* Reset return table
  REFRESH et_return.
* Header text must be populated
  IF is_gohead-bktxt IS INITIAL.
*   Configure message, warning
    ls_bapiret-type    = 'W'.
    ls_bapiret-id      = 'ZMB'.
    ls_bapiret-number  = '060'.
    APPEND ls_bapiret TO et_return.
  ENDIF.

* Item text must be filled
  IF is_goitem-sgtxt IS INITIAL.
*   Configure message, error
```

```
      ls_bapiret-type     = 'E'.
      ls_bapiret-id       = 'ZMB'.
      ls_bapiret-number   = '061'.
      APPEND ls_bapiret TO et_return.
    ENDIF.
  ENDMETHOD.
ENDMETHOD.
```

Listing 5.25 Coding on the Method ITEM_MODIFY

5.4 Check of the Earliest Delivery Date

You have the option in the purchase order to specify a delivery date. However, vendors often don't keep to the delivery date and deliver goods too early. When this is better controlled, you can set the message M7 254 ("Earliest Possible Delivery Date is &" as shown in Figure 5.7) as an error message in Customizing. To do this, choose the MATERIALS MANAGEMENT • INVENTORY MANAGEMENT AND PHYSICAL INVENTORY • DEFINE ATTRIBUTES OF SYSTEM MESSAGES • SETTINGS FOR SYSTEM MESSAGES setting in Transaction SPRO, and define the message M7 254 as type 'E'.

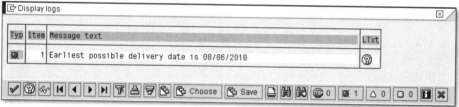

Figure 5.7 Error Message M7 254

As a result, all goods receipts that are supposed to be posted at an earlier date are rejected with the error message. However, you can post the goods receipt in the GR blocked stock (transaction type 103).

In certain circumstances, the settings for such an error message are too strict. With the enhancement MEFLD004 (EXIT_SAPLEINR_004), you can specify the earliest delivery date. Let's assume you have activated the error message. Vendor 1002 is allowed to deliver before the delivery date specified in the purchase order, but not before the purchase order date. The following applies to all other vendors: For all items with material group 00, a delivery of up to seven days prior to the delivery date is possible. For other goods deliveries, a delivery of up to three days prior to the delivery date is permitted.

1. Create a new project in Transaction CMOD, and include the enhancement MEFLD004.

2. Switch to the user exit EXIT_SAPLEINR_004, and create the include ZXM06U54.

3. In the interface of the exit, the purchase order header (EKKO) and the purchase order item to be checked (EKPO) are transferred. Based on this data, you can overwrite the earliest delivery date (parameter FRLFD). The field FRLFD already contains the delivery date from the purchase order. You can therefore leave the content unchanged, if no special rule applies.

   Check whether the vendor (EKKO-LIFNR) has the number 1002 (look out for leading zeros); if yes, the purchase order date (EKKO-BEDAT) will apply as the earliest delivery date.

4. Check whether the purchase order item has the material group 003; if yes, a goods receipt of up to seven days prior to the delivery date is expected to be possible. Because the field FRLFD already contains the delivery date from the purchase order, you can simply deduct seven days.

   For all other items, the goods receipt can take place three days earlier. Also carry out the respective calculation (see Listing 5.26). Don't forget to activate the project so that your user exit will run.

```
*&---------------------------------------------------------------------*
*&  Include           ZXM06U54
*&---------------------------------------------------------------------*
*"*"Local interface:
*"  IMPORTING
*"     VALUE(EKKO) TYPE   EKKO
*"     VALUE(EKPO) TYPE   EKPO
*"  CHANGING
*"     VALUE(FRLFD) LIKE  EBEFU-FRLFD
*"---------------------------------------------------------------------
* Determine earliest delivery date dynamically

IF ekko-lifnr = '0000001002'.
* Vendor 1002 is allowed to deliver earlier indefinitely,
* however, not before the purchase order date
  frlfd = ekko-bedat.
```

```
ELSE.
* Item for material group 003?
  IF ekpo-matkl = '003'.
*   Goods receipt can take place seven days earlier
    frlfd = frlfd - 7.
  ELSE.
*   Goods receipt can take place three days earlier
    frlfd = frlfd - 3.
  ENDIF.
ENDIF.
```

Listing 5.26 Coding on User-Exit EXIT_SAPLEINR_004

5.5 Tolerance Limits for Scheduling Agreements

Using the current date, the default quantity and tolerance check quantity are determined from the schedule lines when goods receipts are posted according to scheduling agreements. If no tolerances are permitted in the scheduling agreement, and the vendor occasionally delivers a few days too early, you receive an error message in the goods receipt (see Figure 5.8).

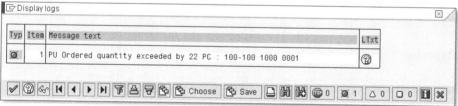

Figure 5.8 Exceeding the Tolerance Levels

If your vendor is allowed to deliver the goods, for example, up to three days earlier, you may use the user exit EXIT_SAPLEINR_001 of the enhancement MEVME001 to determine the default quantity and tolerance levels dynamically.

5.5.1 Overwriting Overdelivery Quantity

Let's first take a look at the scheduling agreement schedule in Figure 5.9. Items 1 and 2 have each a scheduled quantity of 10 pieces. A goods receipt of more than 12 pieces has already been posted. Item 1 is therefore complete; for item 2, there is still an open quantity of 8 pieces.

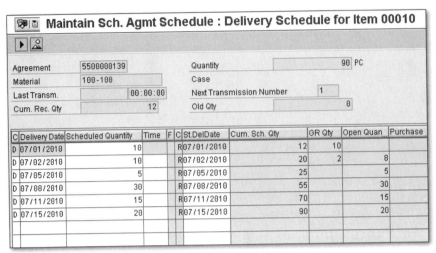

Figure 5.9 Scheduling Agreement Schedule

On July 6, 2010, another goods receipt of more than 43 pieces is now supposed to be posted. The open quantity consists of the 5 pieces scheduled for delivery on July 5, 2010, and also of the 8 pieces still open from the previous items. A total of 13 pieces are open. The goods receipt is therefore rejected due to an overbooking of 30 pieces (43 pc – 13 pc). The vendor has already added the 30 pieces, which are expected on July 8, 2010 — that is, in the future. Because this is within the 3 days for which you allow an earlier delivery, the goods receipt is expected to go through.

1. To resolve this situation, you must program the aforementioned user exit EXIT_ SAPLEINR_001. Create a project in Transaction CMOD, and add the enhancement MEVME001.

2. Switch to the user exit EXIT_SAPLEINR_001, and create the include ZXM06U28.

3. You get two parameters in the interface: The parameter POT contains the item data from the scheduling agreement; the internal table CETT contains all schedule lines. Based on this data, you can perform your own calculations and fill the parameters according to Table 5.12. Keep in mind that these parameters in the documentation on the enhancement MEVME001 are not completely and uniquely defined. The parameters F3 and F4 have only been added with SAP Note 737495; the documentation has not been customized, however.

Parameter	Description
F1	WE default quantity
F2	Open quantity on key date
F3	Underdelivery quantity
F4	Overdelivery quantity

Table 5.12 Output Parameter EXIT_SAPLEINR_001

4. Because the overdelivery quantity is customized, you need to determine a new value for parameter F4. The calculation for this works very simply. The parameter contains the complete scheduled quantity, starting from the first item of the scheduling to the last scheduling prior to the key data in total. The system automatically deducts goods receipts already carried out, so you don't need to take this into consideration.

Calculate in a loop via Table CETT the total of all schedule quantities with one vendor smaller than the date "today + 3 days". You write the result of the calculation in the field F4 (see Listing 5.27).

```
*&---------------------------------------------------------------*
*&  Include          ZXM06U28
*&---------------------------------------------------------------*
*"*"Local interface:
*"  IMPORTING
*"     VALUE(POT)
*"  TABLES
*"       CETT STRUCTURE   EKET
*"  CHANGING
*"     VALUE(F1)
*"     VALUE(F2)
*"     VALUE(F3) OPTIONAL
*"     VALUE(F4) OPTIONAL
*"--------------------------------------------------------------
* Local declarations
DATA lv_menge TYPE eket-menge.
DATA lv_checkdate TYPE eket-eindt.

* Consider schedules until today + 3 days
lv_checkdate = sy-datlo + 3.

* Total all schedule quantities
```

```
LOOP AT cett WHERE eindt <= lv_checkdate.
  lv_menge = lv_menge + cett-menge.
ENDLOOP.

* Transfer of the calculated value as maximum limit
f4 = lv_menge.
```

Listing 5.27 Coding for EXIT_SAPLEINR_001

5.5.2 Overwriting Default Quantity

After the goods receipt that includes 43 pieces has been posted, the new situation in the scheduling agreement is shown in Figure 5.10. As you can see, if there is no longer any quantity open until and including July 8, 2010, the next goods receipt is not expected again until July 11, 2010.

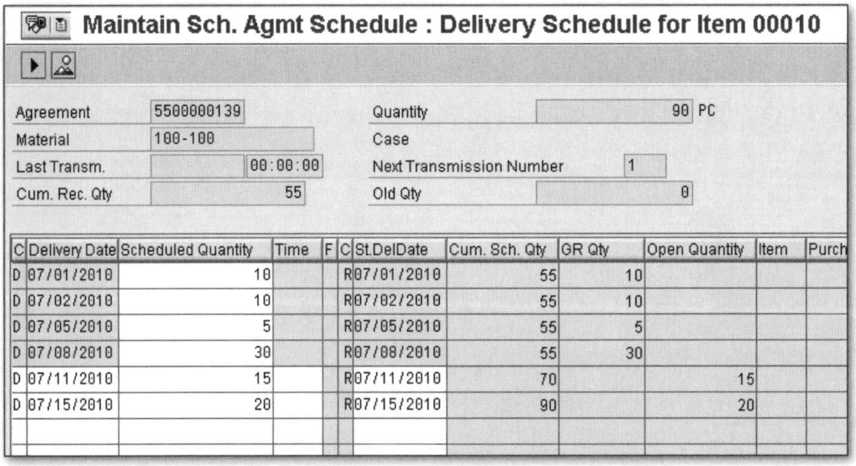

C	Delivery Date	Scheduled Quantity	Time	F	C	St.DelDate	Cum. Sch. Qty	GR Qty	Open Quantity	Item	Purch
D	07/01/2010	10			R	07/01/2010	55	10			
D	07/02/2010	10			R	07/02/2010	55	10			
D	07/05/2010	5			R	07/05/2010	55	5			
D	07/08/2010	30			R	07/08/2010	55	30			
D	07/11/2010	15			R	07/11/2010	70		15		
D	07/15/2010	20			R	07/15/2010	90		20		

Figure 5.10 Scheduling Agreement Schedule following Goods Receipt

If you now receive a new delivery of more than 15 pieces on July 11, 2010, and these are supposed to be posted as goods receipt, you receive the message "Document contains no selectable item" if the user hasn't activated the PROPOSE ALL ITEMS option. You can react using the user exit: If an open scheduling exists within the next three days, the first open quantity found is suggested. In the example given, this quantity refers to the 15 pieces from July 11, 2010.

1. Navigate again to the user exit `EXIT_SAPLEINR_001`, and enhance the coding for the current case. The field `F2` contains the quantity of all schedulings up to and

including today, minus the goods receipts already carried out. If this value is zero, the line is not suggested. Check the value F2. If no quantity is suggested here, you must calculate a new value.

2. Because the system has already checked all schedulings up to and including the current date, you must check Table CETT again in a loop only from the day "today + 1" until "today + 3". The schedule quantity, as before in the field MENGE, was carried out in the goods receipts in field WEMNG. Calculate the open quantity from this. As soon as you find an open quantity, you can leave the loop.

3. You don't need to assign the result of the calculation to the field F2. In fact, the field F1 again contains the complete schedule quantity from the first day of the scheduling agreement until today. The system deducts the goods receipts already carried out only later from this figure. Simply add the result of your calculation to the field F1. The line with your determined quantity is therefore suggested (see Listing 5.28).

```
...
* Additional determination of the default quantity
* Further data declarations
DATA lv_morgen TYPE eket-eindt.

IF F2 = 0.
* No default quantity available, check whether an open
* schedule exists in the period today + 1 until today + 3
  lv_morgen = sy-datlo + 1.
  clear lv_menge.

  LOOP AT cett WHERE eindt <= lv_checkdate AND
                     eindt >= lv_morgen.
    lv_menge = cett-menge - cett-wemng.
    IF lv_menge > 0.
*     Open schedule available, exit loop
      EXIT.
    ENDIF.
  ENDLOOP.

* Increase expected quantity for found value
  F1 = F1 + lv_menge.

ENDIF.
```

Listing 5.28 Further Coding for EXIT_SAPLEINR_001

4. Based on the situation from Figure 5.10, if you post a goods receipt on July 10, 2010, an item with a quantity of 15 pieces is suggested to you, which is the value of the schedule of July 11, 2010.

5.6 Enhancement of Reservations

For reservations, you can't use Transaction MIGO. As previously stated, reservations are created or changed in Transactions MB21 and MB22. Therefore, you can't use any enhancements for reservations, for example, the BAdI MB_MIGO_BADI, to prepopulate fields or to carry out input checks. Even here there is some assistance — the BAdI MB_RESERVATION_BADI.

This BAdI is essentially suitable for two situations. First, there is the method DATA_MODIFY, which is called when an item is entered before the detail screen view (see Figure 5.11) is displayed. You can use this method to prepopulate individual fields with values. The method DATA_CHECK is then called. Here you have the option to carry out custom checks and display, if applicable, a warning or error message.

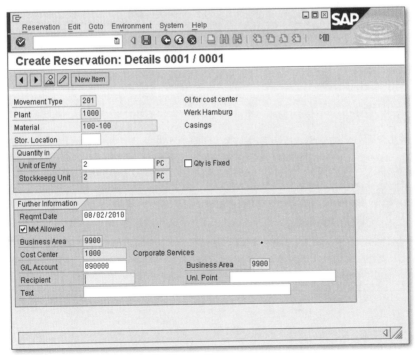

Figure 5.11 Detailed Entry in the Reservation

For both cases, a small example will help you implement these enhancements.

5.6.1 Prepopulating Fields

The prepopulation of fields via the method `DATA_MODIFY` works relatively simply. However, you can't overwrite all of the fields of the document. All fields of Table 5.13 can basically be overwritten. However, this list is further restricted by the current field status. Fields that haven't been integrated may also not be overwritten by the BAdI method. Therefore, internal Table `IT_CHANGEABLE` is transferred as a parameter that contains all changeable fields. All changes you make in the BAdI to fields not contained there are subsequently not copied.

Field	Description
RESB-MATNR	Material number
RESB-WERKS	Plant
RESB-LGORT	Storage location
RESB-CHARG	Batch
RESB-SAKNR	GL account number
RESB-ERFMG	Quantity in unit of entry
RESB-ERFMG	Unit of entry
RESB-BDMNG	Requirement quantity
RESB-FMENG	Characteristic: Fixed quantity
RESB-KZEAR	Characteristic: Final issue of the reservation
RESB-XLOEK	Item deleted
RESB-WEMPF	Ship-to party
RESB-ABLAD	Unloading point
RESB-SGTXT	Item text
RESB-BDMNG	Requirement date of the components
RESB-XWAOK	Characteristic: Goods movement to the reservation permitted

Table 5.13 Fields of the Reservation that Can Be Overwritten

Furthermore, the parameter `I_NEW_ITEM` exists, which means that this item will run the first time in the method. If your prepopulation is only supposed to be a suggestion that can be overwritten by the user at any time via other values, then it makes sense to check this parameter and to overwrite the field content only when it is run for the first time.

You can find the complete parameter interface of the method DATA_MODIFY in Table 5.14.

Parameter	Description
IT_CHANGEABLE	Table of the changeable fields.
I_NEW_ITEM	Current item is new and is handled the first time in the method.
CS_RKPF	Header data of the reservation. The fields of this structure cannot be changed.
CS_RESB	Structure on an item of the reservation; the fields contained may be overwritten if the field is contained in Table IT_CHANGEABLE.

Table 5.14 Parameters of the Method DATA_MODIFY

In a small example, the field GL account (RESB-SAKNR) is populated for all reservations in plant 1000 with the GL account number 400000.

1. Create an implementation for the BAdI MB_RESERVATION_BADI in Transaction SE19. You can choose, for example, ZMB_RESERVATION_BADI as the name of the implementation.

2. Now navigate to the method DATA_MODIFY. The GL account is only a default value that can be overwritten by the user at any time. For this reason, the method is executed for an item only on the first run (i.e., before the detail screen for an item may have been displayed the first time). Therefore, check the content of I_NEW_ITEM, and exit the method if necessary.

3. Next, you must check whether the field may at all be changed. For this, check whether the field is available in Table IT_CHANGEABLE.

   This internal table is defined via a table type TDTAB_C132 in the ABAP Dictionary; however, this is done without using a structure but instead via an integrated data type. For this reason, the only field of this internal table doesn't have any defined name. However, you can always access the internal table via the field name TABLE_LINE.

4. When the checks are successful, you can overwrite the field value in the structure CS_RESB. A suitable example is given in Listing 5.29.

```
METHOD if_ex_mb_reservation_badi~data_modify .
* Prepopulate GL account
* Prepopulation is only to be a default value, therefore
* only execute item on first run
  CHECK i_new_item IS NOT INITIAL.

* Check whether GL account is changeable
  READ TABLE it_changeable WITH KEY table_line = 'RESB-SAKNR'
  TRANSPORTING NO FIELDS.

* Suggest GL account for plant 1000
  IF sy-subrc = 0 AND
     cs_resb-werks = '1000'.
     cs_resb-saknr = '400000'.
  ENDIF.
ENDMETHOD.
```
Listing 5.29 Coding on the Method DATA_MODIFY

5.6.2 Checking Entries

Custom input checks are also simple to implement. To implement your checks, the header and item data are provided. To trigger a warning or error message, you can work perfectly normally with the MESSAGE command, but you must trigger the exception EXTERNAL_MESSAGE.

You can find the parameter interface of the method DATA_CHECK in Table 5.15.

Parameter	Description
IT_CHANGEABLE	This internal table again contains the list of current changeable fields. This doesn't usually play any major role for this method.
IS_RKPF	The header data of the reservation.
IS_RESB	Structure on an item of the reservation.
I_NEW_ITEM	Current item is new and is handled the first time in the method.

Table 5.15 Parameters of the Method DATA_CHECK

As an example, the fields are supposed to be checked for the ship-to party (RESB-WEMPF) and the unloading point (RESB-ABLAD). The specification of a ship-to party is mandatory. If this specification is missing, it must be confirmed by an error message. If there is no entry in the unloading point field, this is indicated by a warning message.

1. Navigate to the implementation of the BAdIs that you created in the previous example on method DATA_MODIFY. Then, switch to the method DATA_CHECK.

2. The method is only called for an item when the item is new or has been changed. Therefore, the evaluation of the parameter I_NEW_ITEM isn't absolutely necessary. Check whether the ship-to party is filled, and display an error message. To trigger the exception, you need the addition RAISING EXTERNAL_MESSAGE.

3. So that the message only appears for the unloading point, which is just a warning when the item is entered, but not in the case of each subsequent change, you can at this point also check the parameter I_NEW_ITEM. If the parameter is set, and the unloading point hasn't been completed, a warning message is displayed. You must also use the addition RAISING EXTERNAL_MESSAGE with regard to warning messages.

By displaying the warning message, you can always navigate to the detail screen in which the unloading point can be entered. This is usually only shown when an important piece of information is missing. You can find the relevant example in Listing 5.30.

```
METHOD if_ex_mb_reservation_badi~data_check .
* The ship-to party must be filled.
  IF is_resb-wempf is initial.
*   Message: "Please specify a ship-to party"
    MESSAGE  e100(ZMM) RAISING external_message.
  ENDIF.


* The unloading point should be filled
* Check only on initial run of item
  IF i_new_item is not initial AND
     is_resb-ablad IS INITIAL.
*   Message: "Unloading point was not entered!"
    MESSAGE  w101(ZMM) RAISING external_message.
  ENDIF.
ENDMETHOD.
```

Listing 5.30 Coding on the Method DATA_CHECK

6   User Exits and BAdIs in the Valuation and Account Assignment Area

The settings for the valuation and account assignment aren't part of any special area in MM, but they are commonly used. The main topics at this point are how stocks are valued and how transactions are posted to accounts in Financial Accounting (FI).

The current enhancements in the valuation area and account assignment area are rather simple and are used to influence the balance sheet valuation or the determination of lowest value. The possible customizations are so customer-specific here that it hardly makes any sense to present one of these enhancements in detail. However, the enhancement used to individually control the GR/IR account (clearing account between goods receipts and invoice receipts) is frequently required by customers, so we'll be working with this enhancement in this chapter.

6.1   GR/IR Clearing Account

The GR/IR clearing account is posted to a purchase order upon goods receipt and is again credited at a later point when posting the incoming invoice. Therefore, you can view in this account how many incoming invoices are still outstanding on already delivered goods. For this, you usually set a clearing account for a transaction key WRX in the account determination that is used for all respective postings.

You may want to use different GR/IR accounts due to specific dependencies. For example, you might want to manage a custom GR/IR account for each of your purchasing organizations to create differentiated evaluations. You can do this with the enhancement LMR1M002, through which you can set the account modification constant for the transaction key WRX, and choose the GR/IR account. The user exit contained is called once with GR postings and incoming invoices for each purchase order item; that is, you can have completely different GR/IR accounts within a document.

To use the account modification constant and several accounts, you must maintain the respective settings in the Customizing of the account determination. All necessary customizing steps can be found in Transaction SPRO via the MATERIALS MANAGEMENT • VALUATION AND ACCOUNT ASSIGNMENT • ACCOUNT DETERMINATION • ACCOUNT DETERMINATION WITHOUT WIZARD path.

1. Choose the Customizing point SET AUTOMATIC POSTINGS, and then click ACCOUNT ASSIGNMENT. You can also directly access the maintenance via Transaction OBYC.

2. Scroll to Transaction WRX, and then double-click the respective line. You may be asked for the chart of accounts for which the maintenance is supposed to be carried out. Choose the chart of accounts that is assigned to your company code.

3. If the column GEN. MODIFICATION (i.e., an account modification constant) isn't yet displayed, click RULES (make a note of the currently set accounts beforehand).

4. Highlight the GEN. MODIFICATION option in the ACCOUNTS ARE SPECIFIED DEPENDING ON area, and save this change. You now get a warning message that the current specification of accounts is deleted. Confirm this warning.

5. Enter the previously noted account settings again, and leave the GEN. MODIFICATION column empty. This entry is used for the account determination when the user exit doesn't return any different account modification constant. You will receive the same warning message as before.

6. You can now maintain other accounts by using different account modification constants (see Figure 6.1).

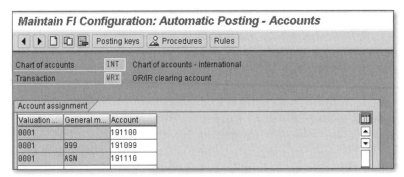

Figure 6.1 Setting Different GR/IR Accounts

6.2 Overriding the Account Determination in the User Exit

The purchase number (I_WRXMOD-EBELN) and the purchase order item (I_WRXMOD-EBELP) are transferred to the user exit EXIT_SAPLKONT_011. Using these parameters, you can read the complete purchase order data. You can then determine the account modification constant depending on the purchase order data and then transfer this to the output parameter E_KONTO_MODIF. You can also leave this output parameter empty to use the standard account.

No Queries in the Transaction Code

You can specify the GR/IR account in this user exit depending on the purchase order data in this user exit via the account modification. However, no logical check takes place here, which means you are responsible for debiting the same account that is credited with an incoming invoice for a purchase order item in the GR.

Therefore, you should not execute any queries in your coding in the transaction code; that is, no other account modification constant is provided in transactions of Inventory Management when you do this in transactions of Logistics Invoice Verification. Otherwise, you don't have any GR in an account that is never balanced, and you have a negative balance in another account because this account was never debited with a GR.

The user exits are programmed using the following steps. You can also see in Listing 6.1 how you can determine different data from the purchase order, even if not all of the data determined is used for the specific example. You can see the listing as a sample that you can customize for your own individual requirements. All purchase order data are documented in detail in the coding.

1. Navigate to Transaction CMOD, and create a project, for example, ZMR1M002.

2. Assign the enhancement LMR1M002 to this project.

3. Now switch to components, and navigate to the user exit EXIT_SAPLKONT_011. Overwrite the account modification constant with the desired value. You can use Listing 6.1 as a sample for this.

```
*---------------------------------------------------------------*
*    INCLUDE ZXM08U18
*---------------------------------------------------------------*
*"*"Local interface:
*"  IMPORTING
*"     VALUE(I_WRXMOD) LIKE  WRXMOD STRUCTURE  WRXMOD
*"  EXPORTING
```

```
*"      VALUE(E_KONTO_MODIF) LIKE  T030-KOMOK
*--------------------------------------------------------------*


* Data collection to obtain data of purchase order:
DATA: ls_ekko TYPE ekko,
      ls_ekpo TYPE ekpo,
      ls_ekpa TYPE ekpa,
      lt_konv TYPE TABLE OF konv,
      ls_konv TYPE konv.


* Read purchase order header
SELECT SINGLE * FROM ekko
               INTO ls_ekko
               WHERE ebeln = i_wrxmod-ebeln.


* Read purchase order item
SELECT SINGLE * FROM ekpo
               INTO ls_ekpo
               WHERE ebeln = i_wrxmod-ebeln AND
                     ebelp = i_wrxmod-ebelp.


* Read partner data
* Example header – invoicing party (in ls_ekpa-lifn2)
SELECT SINGLE * FROM ekpa
               INTO ls_ekpa
               WHERE ebeln = i_wrxmod-ebeln AND
                     ebelp = '00000'         AND
                     parvw = 'RS'.              "Partnerrolle


* Read conditions
SELECT * FROM konv INTO TABLE lt_konv
               WHERE knumv = ls_ekko-knumv AND
                     kposn = i_wrxmod-ebelp.
* Internal table lt_konv now contains all conditions
* for item:
* LT_KONV-KSCHL = Condition Key
* LT_KONV-LIFNR = Freight vendor with corresponding conditions
* Set account modification constant
* Example: dependent on purchasing organization
CASE ls_ekko-ekorg.
  WHEN '0001'.
    e_konto_modif = '999'.
  WHEN '1000'.
```

```
      e_konto_modif = 'ASN'.
  WHEN OTHERS.
     CLEAR e_konto_modif.
ENDCASE.
```

Listing 6.1 Sample for the User Exit EXIT_SAPLKONT_011

4. Don't forget to activate your project so that the coding is implemented. If you now perform a posting on purchasing organization 1000, the ASN account modification constant is set, and the different account 191110 is therefore posted (see Figure 6.2).

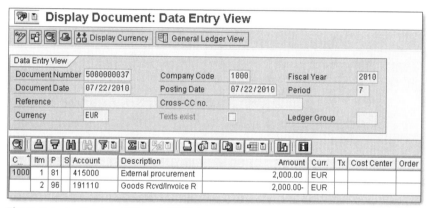

Figure 6.2 Posting to a Different GR/IR Account

7   User Exits and BAdIs in Logistics Invoice Verification

An extensive range of user exits and BAdIs are available in Logistics Invoice Verification, that is, the entry of incoming invoices in MM. However, for some time, it wasn't possible to connect custom fields to an invoice document in Transaction MIRO without modifying the system (see the upcoming box: Custom Fields via Modification). This has changed with the technical Basis SAP ERP Central Component 6.0. There finally exists a proper solution to integrate a custom subscreen in the form of a BAdI. Nevertheless, this also has its pitfalls. For this reason, the usage of this BAdI will take up much of this chapter. This is described in Section 7.1, Custom Fields in Transaction MIRO.

In Section 7.2, Overriding Tolerance Checks, you can also find an enhancement with which you can dynamically overwrite the settings of the tolerance check in Customizing.

7.1   Custom Fields in Transaction MIRO

With the BAdI `MRM_ITEM_CUSTFIELDS`, there is an option from SAP ERP Central Component 6.0 to integrate a custom subscreen at an item level in the invoice document. This section describes step-by-step how to use this BAdI and how communication with your subscreen works.

Custom Fields via Modification

If you use a release prior to SAP ECC 6.0, you can also implement custom fields via modification. The procedure for this is described in SAP Notes 352701 (Document Item) and 174413 (G/L Account Tab). These notes describe how a field can be added by modifying the standard dynpros and ABAP Dictionary structures.

You must also pay attention to fields in the G/L ACCOUNT tab — the field with an identical name must be attached as an append structure to Table BSEG or it can't be saved in the database.

The field must also be included in some control tables. You can access this via Transaction OXK3. Here you choose the ACCOUNT ASSIGNMENT FIELDS • EXPERT MODE menu. Then expand the CUSTOMER-DEFINED ACCOUNT ASSIGNMENTS • CUSTOMER INCLUDE STRUCTURE • CI_COBL area. Now move the cursor on the field concerned and choose the ACCOUNT ASSIGNMENT FIELD • ADD CONTROL ENTRIES • TEST RUN or UPDATE RUN menu option.

7.1.1 Overview of the Solution via BAdI

To map custom fields in the invoice document (see Figure 7.1), you need several elements. To gain a better overview, you find a rough view of the processes in this sub-chapter.

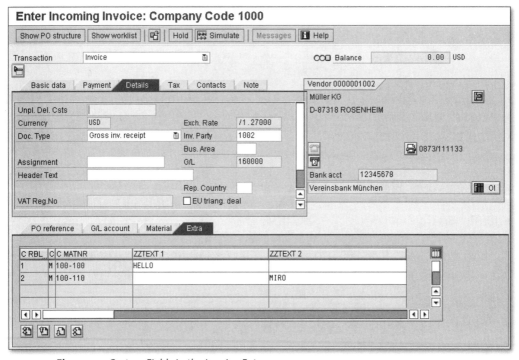

Figure 7.1 Custom Fields in the Invoice Entry

Follow these steps:

1. Define the actual dynpro that is to appear as a subscreen in the invoice document. Please note, however, that this subscreen must map all available document

items. This means that you must create a table control in a custom dynpro in a Z-program together with the necessary flow logic.

2. The subscreen must then be announced to the invoice document, so you must enter the name of the previously created program and the dynpro number in the BAdI implementation. You must also specify a name for the tabstrip. This takes place in the BAdI method TABPAGE_LABEL_SET.

If you activate the BAdI implementation now, these two steps are already sufficient to allow the subscreen to appear on the screen, when, for example, Transaction MIRO is started. Additionally, the new input fields wouldn't have any further function.

3. The fields that are copied from your subscreen to the invoice document must be created in the ABAP Dictionary structure CI_DRSEG_CUST. This structure is already a component of the structure DRSEG_CI, which in turn is assigned to the structure DRSEG. DRSEG is the central structure that maps all item fields of an invoice document.

To store the fields also in the database, the fields with an identical name must be attached as an append to the respective database table.

4. Now it's time to bring the BAdI methods to life. The main task of the methods is to establish communication between the item structure DRSEG and your dynpro. For this, the previously mentioned methods are automatically called in Table 7.1 in the called sequence.

Step	Method/Time	Description
1.	CUSTOMDATA_MODIFY	This is the first called method of the BAdI. It is implemented as soon as the custom tabstrip has been selected. You can use this method to prepopulate custom fields with data.
2.	INVOICE_DATA_TRANSFER	This method runs next. Here, you prepare the data, which is to be displayed in the dynpro, in the attributes of the class.
3.	Display of the dynpro	The dynpro is now displayed and can be maintained by the user.
4.	CUSTOM_DATA_GET	As soon as the user triggers an action, this method is called. Here, you must retrieve the data prepared and possibly changed by the dynpro and write back to the data model.

Table 7.1 BAdI Call in a Dialog Step

5. Finally, you must still customize the flow logic of your dynpro to transfer or return the previously prepared data to the table control. To do this, call the two remaining methods of the BAdI from the flow logic. These methods are not automatically started at a specified place but are used for data exchange with your dynpro. You can find the exact procedure for this in Table 7.2.

Time	Description
PROCESS BEFORE OUTPUT (PBO)	As soon as this part of the flow logic is started, you must retrieve the data to be displayed. To do this, call the method INVOICE_DATA_GET from the PBO. This method provides you with the data that you have already prepared via INVOICE_DATA_TRANSFER.
PROCESS AFTER INPUT (PAI)	After the user has triggered a dialog step, check whether there has been any change. You write back the new data to the BAdI (to later further process the data in CUSTOM_DATA_GET) by calling the method CUSTOM_DATA_TRANSFER.

Table 7.2 Overview of Flow Logic of Your Dynpro

As soon as you've implemented these steps, you can use your custom fields and save these together with your document. In the following sections, we'll look at this procedure in detail again.

7.1.2 BAdI in Detail — Customizations in the ABAP Dictionary

In the following example, the two fields ZZTEXT_1 and ZZTEXT_2 are entered and saved per item. Fields in the customer namespace should always start with a double Z. Both fields use the data element CHAR32 that is available in every system.

As already described, the fields must first be included in the work structure DRSEG, which is used for all items in the invoice document. The structure DRSEG already contains an include DRSEG_CI with three defined fields and the include structure CI_DRSEG_CUST. You can include your custom fields in this structure.

1. Navigate to the ABAP DictionaryABAP Dictionary (Transaction SE11), and edit the structure CI_DRSEG_CUST (select DATA TYPE). This structure isn't usually available yet. You need to create it. Switch to the edit mode.

2. Enter the two fields `ZZTEXT_1` and `ZZTEXT_2`, and use in each case the data element `CHAR32`.

3. You can define the category CANNOT BE ENHANCED via the EXTRAS • ENHANCEMENT CATEGORY menu. It doesn't matter too much if you don't do this. You will, however, receive a warning message on activation.

4. Save and activate your structure. It may take some time until it is activated because all objects using the structure `DRSEG` are also regenerated.

5. Look at the structure `DRSEG_CI`. This should contain the fields as shown in Table 7.3. As you can see, besides your custom fields, the structure also contains the item number to which your fields belong. Using the number, this structure accurately describes a line of the document from your custom fields' point of view. You will therefore use this structure more frequently later on.

Field Name	Description
C_RBLGP	Item number of the document
C_KOART	Account type: ▶ A: Appendices ▶ D: Debtors ▶ K: Creditors ▶ M: Material ▶ S: GL accounts
C_MATNR	Material number in account type M
ZZTEXT_1	Your first custom field
ZZTEXT_2	Your second custom field

Table 7.3 Structure DRSEG_CI

All prerequisites are now fulfilled to subsequently work with your fields within the BAdI and in your dynpro. So that the data is also saved in the database, you need to also attach the fields via append to the respective table. In Table 7.4, you can see all the options provided for this.

Table/Structure	Description
RSEG	Database table to store the document items.
RBDRSEG	Database table to temporarily store the document items in the background check.
RBMA	Database table to store the fields relating to the material.
COBL_MRM	Structure of the account assignment fields (G/L ACCOUNTS tab). Fields that you add to this structure are stored in the database table RBCO.

Table 7.4 Tables for Storing Custom Fields

Because the fields ZZTEXT_1 and ZZTEXT_2 do not display any account assignment information and aren't material-related, they are to be saved in Table RSEG.

1. Display the database table RSEG in the ABAP Dictionary (Transaction SE11). Then click the APPEND STRUCTURE button on the upper-right side.

2. In the selection window that appears, select the CREATE APPEND icon. You can use, for example, ZZRSEG as the name for the append structure.

3. Specify the two fields ZZTEXT_1 and ZZTEXT_2. Make sure that the notation with the field name of the structure CI_DRSEG_CUST is identical. You must also use the same data element (CHAR32) for these fields (see Figure 7.2).

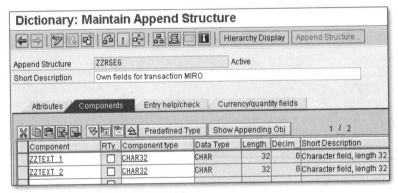

Figure 7.2 Append Structure ZZRSEG

4. Also maintain the enhancement category again here in the EXTRAS • ENHANCEMENT CATEGORY menu as CANNOT BE ENHANCED.

5. Save and activate the append structure.

When you use the background check and enter documents via Transaction MIRA, which you then further process and schedule to the background check via Transaction MIR6 or MIR4, the item data is temporarily saved in Table RBDRSEG. Only when the background check (Transaction MRBP) has been run with an error are the records deleted again from Table RBDRSEG and saved in Table RSEG.

So that the custom fields can be entered at any time in this procedure, you should also enhance Table RBDRSEG identically with Table RSEG custom fields.

7.1.3 Creating a Custom Dynpro with Table Control

Next, you also need the dynpro that will be integrated as a subscreen into the tabstrip. You ideally pack this into a custom program in the form of a function group or in a report of the type MODULE POOL.

1. Start Transaction SE80, and create a new program. For the sake of the example, the name SAPMZMRM and program type MODULE POOL have been used (see Figure 7.3).

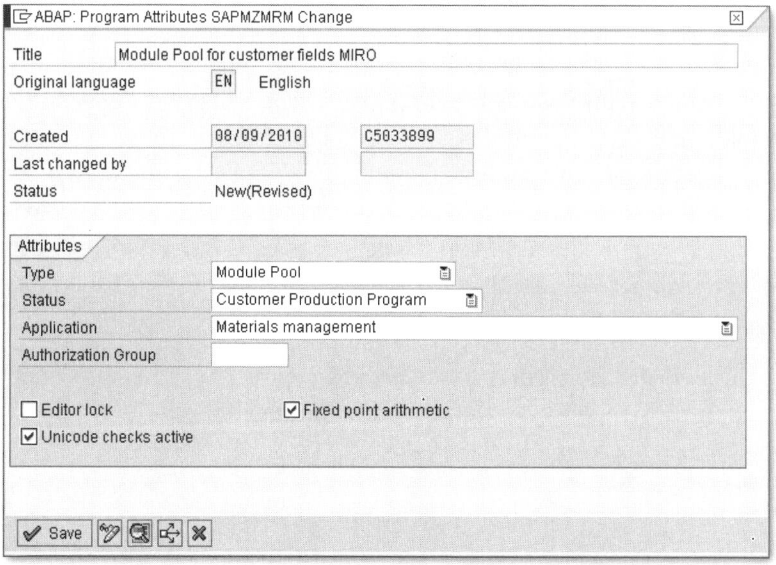

Figure 7.3 Module Pool for Inclusion of the Dynpro

2. Before you generate the dynpro with the table control, you should consider which fields will be displayed in the table control. You need an internal table and a work structure for these tables to supply the table control with data.

   You can simply use the structure DRSEG_CI. Besides your custom fields, this also contains the item number and is therefore ideal for displaying onscreen. For this reason, create two global data objects in program SAPMZMRM as shown in Listing 7.1.

   ```
   PROGRAM  sapmzmrm.

   * Global data for table control
   DATA: gs_drseg_ci TYPE drseg_ci,
         gt_drseg_ci TYPE TABLE OF drseg_ci.
   ```
   Listing 7.1 Global Data for Table Control

3. Now activate your program. Then right-click in Transaction SE80 in the Repository Browser on the program name on the left-hand side. In the context menu that appears, choose CREATE • DYNPRO. Specify 0100 as the dynpro number.

4. Give a brief description of this dynpro, and only choose the SUBSCREEN option in the PROPERTIES tabstrip in the DYNPRO TYPE section. Other dynpro types cannot be integrated and you would get a short dump when Transaction MIRO is started.

5. Then switch to the Screen Painter via the LAYOUT icon. First, you generate a table control here using a wizard that saves you a lot of work. To do this, click the TABLE CONTROL (USING WIZARD) icon on the left-hand side, and then draw a box. Start ideally on the top-left side, and draw your table control approximately 100 characters wide and 18 lines high. During the creation, you can see in the upper-right side a counter with the width and height of the table control (see also Figure 7.4).

6. After you've drawn the table control, the wizard appears as shown in Figure 7.5. Skip the initial screen by clicking the NEXT button.

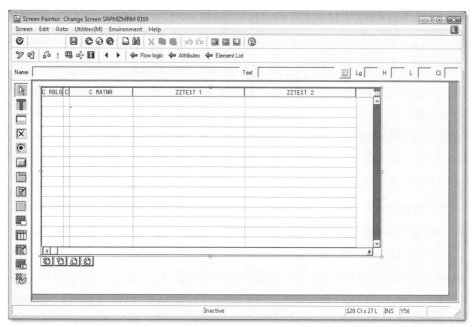

Figure 7.4 Complete Table Control in the Screen Painter

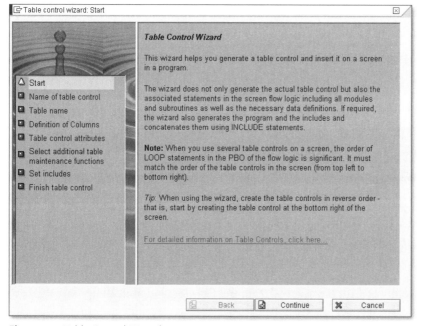

Figure 7.5 Table Control Wizard

7. Specify a clear name in the section NAME OF THE TABLE CONTROL. In the example, TC_MRM_CUST has been used. Click NEXT.

8. In NAME OF THE TABLE choose INTERNAL PROGRAM TABLE as the type, and enter Table GT_DRSEG_CI. Because this internal table doesn't have any header line, you must also activate the TABLE WORK AREA option, and enter the structure GS_DRSEG_CI. Click NEXT.

9. Highlight all of the columns provided in DEFINITION OF THE COLUMNS (which have been copied from the structure DRSEG_CI). Click NEXT.

10. Highlight the INPUT option in the section INPUT/OUTPUT ATTRIBUTES in ATTRIBUTES OF THE TABLE CONTROL. The fields in the standard status are now ready for input. All further options remain unchanged. Click NEXT.

11. You can still activate the option SCROLL in SELECTION OF ADDITIONAL FUNCTIONS FOR THE MAINTENANCE OF TABLES. Four buttons are defined for this below the table control, which the user can use to scroll quickly through the lines of the table control. Click NEXT.

12. In SPECIFY THE INCLUDE, descriptions for various includes are suggested to you, in which the necessary data declarations and flow modules are to be created. Copy the suggestion unchanged, then click NEXT.

13. Click COMPLETE, and all objects and modules necessary for the table control are generated.

14. Save your dynpro, and exit the Screen Painter. Activate the dynpro. Also highlight all other objects that are suggested to you, and activate these as well.

Now you have the fundamental structure of your dynpro. Still missing is the communication with the BAdI to fill the table control with data and write back changed values; however, before you tackle this part, you should first focus on the BAdI.

7.1.4 Preparation of the Data in the BAdI

Now that you've made these preparations, you can deal with the first methods of the BAdI. Refer to Table 7.1 and Table 7.2 again. While the incoming invoices are being processed, the system calls the BAdI methods of Table 7.1. You need to format the data if necessary and temporarily store it in the BAdI. You can store the data in the attributes of the associated class. When you subsequently retrieve the data from the BAdI (see Table 7.2) in the flow logic of your dynpro, the data is ultimately used from these attributes.

1. Create an implementation for the BAdI MRM_ITEM_CUSTFIELDS in Transaction SE19. You can use, for example, ZMRM_ITEM_CUSTFIELDS as the name for the implementation. Save the implementation.

2. Store your previously created dynpro in the implementation by switching to the SUBSCREENS tabstrip and inserting the name and the dynpro number as a called program (see Figure 7.6).

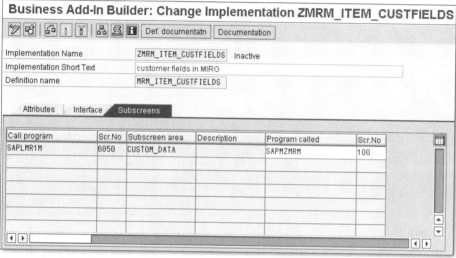

Figure 7.6 The Subscreens Tabstrip of the BAdI Implementation

3. Switch to the INTERFACE tabstrip and navigate by double-clicking in the implementing class (ZCL_IM_MRM_ITEM_CUSTFIELDS).

4. In the class, take a brief look at the ATTRIBUTES tabstrip. You'll find six attributes here (see Table 7.5), which have been automatically created. These attributes have been defined in the interface IF_EX_MRM_ITEM_CUSTFIELDS from which the BAdI has been derived.

An essential basic property of interfaces is that when a class implements an interface (and nothing else is hidden behind the implementation of a BAdI), the class must copy all methods and attributes defined in the interface. For this reason, the attributes are automatically generated at this point. This means you don't have to do anything else. All attributes that you need later are already there!

Attribute	Description
`IF_EX_MRM_ITEM_CUSTFIELDS~` `TRANSACTION_TYPE`	This field contains the transaction type. The most important possible vales are the following: ► A: Display ► H: Add (new document) ► V: Change
`IF_EX_MRM_ITEM_CUSTFIELDS~` `S_RBKPV`	This structure contains all of the document header data.
`IF_EX_MRM_ITEM_CUSTFIELDS~` `TAB_DRSEG`	This internal table contains all the document items data, including your custom fields.
`IF_EX_MRM_ITEM_CUSTFIELDS~` `TAB_DRSEG_CUSTOM`	This internal table only contains your custom fields (type `DRSEG_CI`; refer to Table 7.3).
`IF_EX_MRM_ITEM_CUSTFIELDS~` `H_SORT`	If the sequence of the data records in your dynpro has been changed (sorted), you can set this indicator to retain the sorting.
`IF_EX_MRM_ITEM_CUSTFIELDS~` `H_CHANGE`	Characteristic: The user has changed the custom data.

Table 7.5 Attributes from Interface IF_EX_MRM_ITEM_CUSTFIELDS

5. Switch again to the METHODS tabstrip. First, the methods, which are automatically called, are implemented (refer to Table 7.1). You can use the method `CUSTOMDATA_MODIFY` to prepopulate the custom fields. This is not required for the basic function, however.

Focus instead on the method `INVOICE_DATA_TRANSFER`. This method has four input parameters (transaction type, invoice document header, invoice document items, and your custom fields). In this method, you don't need to do anything but copy the parameters that are transferred here into the attributes of the class. You can find the respective coding for this in Listing 7.2.

```
METHOD if_ex_mrm_item_custfields~invoice_data_transfer.
* Copying of the input parameters in attributes
  me->if_ex_mrm_item_custfields~transaction_type =
      i_transaction_type.
  me->if_ex_mrm_item_custfields~s_rbkpv          =
      is_rbkpv.
  me->if_ex_mrm_item_custfields~tab_drseg        =
```

```
      it_drseg.
  me->if_ex_mrm_item_custfields~tab_drseg_custom =
      it_drseg_custom.
ENDMETHOD.
```

Listing 7.2 Method INVOICE_DATA_TRANSFER

6. After the user has changed the data, it will include the new status in the attribute TAB_DRSEG_CUSTOM (this part is implemented later). The attribute H_CHANGE also contains an indicator to determine whether the data has been changed. In the method CUSTOM_DATA_GET, you now don't need to do anything else but return this information again to the standard program. For the coding, see Listing 7.3.

```
METHOD if_ex_mrm_item_custfields~custom_data_get.
* Return of the changed attributes to callers
  et_drseg_cust =
    me->if_ex_mrm_item_custfields~tab_drseg_custom.
  e_change =
    me->if_ex_mrm_item_custfields~h_change.
ENDMETHOD.
```

Listing 7.3 Method CUSTOM_DATA_GET

7. Follow the methods from Table 7.2, shown earlier. The method INVOICE_DATA_GET is called from the time PROCESS BEFORE OUTPUT of the flow logic of the dynpro. The task of the method is to return the current contents of the attributes on the item data to the dynpro. For this, simply provide the export parameters of the method with the suitable attributes of your class. You can find the coding for this in Listing 7.4.

```
METHOD if_ex_mrm_item_custfields~invoice_data_get.
* Prepare data attributes for dynpro
  e_transaction_type =
      me->if_ex_mrm_item_custfields~transaction_type.
  es_rbkpv            =
      me->if_ex_mrm_item_custfields~s_rbkpv.
  et_drseg            =
      me->if_ex_mrm_item_custfields~tab_drseg.
  et_drseg_cust       =
      me->if_ex_mrm_item_custfields~tab_drseg_custom.
ENDMETHOD.
```

Listing 7.4 Method INVOICE_DATA_GET

8. The method CUSTOM_DATA_TRANSFER will be called from the time PROCESS AFTER INPUT of the flow logic of the dynpro. At this point, the dynpro returns the possibly changed custom fields and an indicator to determine whether any data has been changed. You store this data in the attributes. The previously implemented method CUSTOM_DATA_GET can therefore precisely process this data further (see Listing 7.5).

```
METHOD if_ex_mrm_item_custfields~custom_data_transfer.
  me->if_ex_mrm_item_custfields~tab_drseg_custom =
      it_drseg_cust.
  me->if_ex_mrm_item_custfields~h_change =
      i_change.
ENDMETHOD.
```

Listing 7.5 Method CUSTOM_DATA_TRANSFER

9. Finally, you still need the method TABPAGE_LABEL_SET to give a description to the tabstrip. Use a text symbol so that the description can be translated. A maximum of 11 characters are displayed in the tabstrip (see Listing 7.6).

```
METHOD if_ex_mrm_item_custfields~tabpage_label_set.
* Description of the tabstrip, max. eleven characters
* text-001 contains the text 'addition'
  e_screen_name = text-001.
ENDMETHOD.
```

Listing 7.6 Method TABPAGE_LABEL_SET

7.1.5 Back to the Dynpro

Now that you've also made all preparations in the BAdI, you need to set up the data communication between the BAdI and the dynpro. As previously mentioned, communication between the dynpro and the BAdI flows via the methods INVOICE_DATA_GET and CUSTOM_DATA_TRANSFER, which in turn access the attributes of the class. In object-oriented programming, the content of attributes is in each case precisely linked to an instance of the class. Therefore, if you were to simply generate a new instance on the implementing class ZCL_IM_MRM_ITEM_CUSTFIELDS to subsequently call the aforementioned methods, it would be unsuccessful because the new instance would also have some attributes that would simply be empty.

For this reason, you need to make sure that you access exactly the same instance that has also been used by the BAdI. The static class CL_EXITHANDLER (see Figure 7.7) exists with the method GET_INSTANCE_FOR_SUBSCREENS. You must only transfer an appropriate reference variable to this method that refers to the interface of the BAdI. Using the interface, the method subsequently recognizes the appropriate instance and returns it.

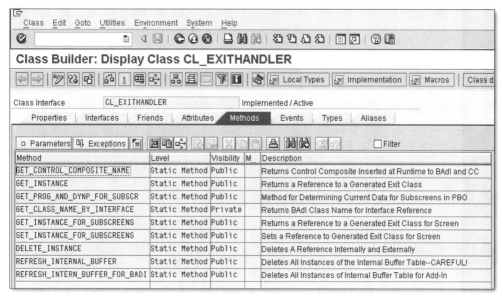

Figure 7.7 Methods of the Class CL_EXITHANDLER

1. Navigate to Transaction SE80 in your program SAPMZMRM, and switch to dynpro 0100. Insert a new MODULE with the name GET_DATA in the flow logic in the time PROCESS BEFORE OUTPUT. Double-click GET_DATA to generate the module. Copy the suggested include (MZMRM_GET_DATA001).

2. Create a new variable in the module as a reference to the interface of the BAdI. You can find the name of the interface in Transaction SE18 or SE19 in the INTER-FACES tabstrip. In this case, the interface is IF_EX_MRM_ITEM_CUSTFIELDS. In the example given, this variable has been named MRM_CUSTFIELDS.

3. Call the method GET_INSTANCE_FOR_SUBSCREENS of the class CL_EXITHANDLER and transfer your previously defined variable. After calling, your variable shows the instance of the BAdI.

4. Retrieve all available data from the BAdI via the method INVOICE_DATA_GET. To include all the data, you must still create suitable variables in your program. Store these variables in the global area so that you can access them at a later stage.

5. Finally, you must transfer the data to your table control. Because the table control uses all of the fields of the structure DRSEG_CI, you can simply copy the content of the internal table ET_DRSEG_CUST, which you obtain in the previous step, to the table GT_DRSEG_CI that supplies your table control. You can find the respective coding for this module in Listing 7.7 and Listing 7.8.

```
PROGRAM  sapmzmrm.
...
* Data declarations for BAdI communication
TYPE-POOLS: mrm, mmcr.

DATA: gv_trtyp LIKE t169-trtyp,
      gs_rbkpv TYPE mrm_rbkpv,
      gt_drseg TYPE mmcr_tdrseg,
      gt_drseg_custom TYPE tdrseg_cust.
```

Listing 7.7 Data Declarations in Program SAPMZMRM

```
*--------------------------------------------------------------*
***INCLUDE MZMRM_GET_DATAO01 .
*--------------------------------------------------------------*
*&      Module  GET_DATA  OUTPUT
*&-----------------------------------------------------------
module GET_DATA output.

* Reference to the interface
DATA: mrm_custfields TYPE REF TO if_ex_mrm_item_custfields.
* Obtain instance
  CALL METHOD cl_exithandler=>get_instance_for_subscreens
    CHANGING
      instance = mrm_custfields
    EXCEPTIONS
      OTHERS  = 6.

* Retrieve data fromBAdI
  CALL METHOD mrm_custfields->invoice_data_get
    IMPORTING
      e_transaction_type = gv_trtyp
      es_rbkpv           = gs_rbkpv
      et_drseg           = gt_drseg
      et_drseg_cust      = gt_drseg_custom.

* Transfer in table control
```

```
    gt_drseg_ci[] = gt_drseg_custom[].

  endmodule.                    " GET_DATA  OUTPUT
```
Listing 7.8 Module GET_DATA

6. Switch back to the flow logic of your dynpro. Create a new module with the name WRITE_DATA as the last module in the time PROCESS AFTER INPUT. Double-click the module name to generate the module, and use the suggested include (MZMRM_WRITE_DATAI01) again.

7. At this point, you must transfer the data back again to the BAdI. No change can fundamentally be made if the user is only in the display mode. You must therefore implement the following checks when the transaction type that you have temporarily saved in GV_TRTYP is not identical to 'A'.

8. You then make a LOOP via the current data of your table control (GT_DRSEG_CI) and compare each line with the original status that has been stored in the PBO in the internal table GT_DRSEG_CUSTOM. If a line has changed, note this, and write the change back to Table GT_DRSEG_CUSTOM.

9. Afterwards, you can create the method CUSTOM_DATA_TRANSFER. The reference variable MRM_CUSTFIELDS defined in the PBO is still available and can therefore be used. Return to Table GT_DRSEG_CUSTOM. If data has been changed, place the indicator I_CHANGE in the parameter interface of the called method. The parameter I_SORT is not used in the example. You can simply return ABAP_FALSE here.

The complete coding for the module WRITE_DATA can be found in Listing 7.9.

```
*--------------------------------------------------------------*
***INCLUDE MZMRM_WRITE_DATAI01 .
*--------------------------------------------------------------*
*&      Module  WRITE_DATA  INPUT
*&-------------------------------------------------------------
MODULE write_data INPUT.

* Local declarations
  DATA lv_change TYPE c.
  DATA ls_drseg_cust TYPE drseg_ci.

* Only when not in display mode
  CHECK gv_trtyp NE 'A'.
```

```
* Have the data been changed?
  LOOP AT gt_drseg_ci INTO gs_drseg_ci.
    READ TABLE gt_drseg_custom
         INTO ls_drseg_cust INDEX sy-tabix.
    IF ls_drseg_cust NE gs_drseg_ci.
*     Data have been changed
      lv_change = 'X'.
      MODIFY gt_drseg_custom FROM gs_drseg_ci
             INDEX sy-tabix.
    ENDIF.
  ENDLOOP.


* Write back data
  CALL METHOD mrm_custfields->custom_data_transfer
    EXPORTING
      i_sort        = abap_false
      it_drseg_cust = gt_drseg_custom
      i_change      = lv_change.

ENDMODULE.                  " WRITE_DATA  INPUT
```
Listing 7.9 Module WRITE_DATA

You should now activate your latest changes and make sure that the BAdI implementation is active. After that, you can test the new function using Transaction MIRO. Both the additional tabstrip and the data you entered should now be displayed.

However, it isn't ideal that all fields are always ready for input. It's better when the three standard fields: The item number, the account type, and the material number (see Table 7.3), aren't fundamentally ready for input. You should also take into account that your custom fields are also deactivated if a mere display transaction accesses these. Also, the user can enter values in new items. Because your custom fields are item related, the input is only possible if an item is actually available in the document. This can be simply checked via the field C_RBLGP — if there is no item number available here, no input is possible.

1. Switch once again to the flow logic of your dynpro. The Table Control Wizard has already suggested a module to you that you can use to change the attributes of the fields (TC_MRM_CUST_CHANGE_FIELD_ATTR).

2. Remove the comments prior to this line, and double-click the name to create the module. Because this is another PBO module on the table control, you can create it in the existing include MZMRMO01.

3. You can then change the fields there, as described earlier. Because this isn't any special technique of the BAdI but belongs to the general programming of table controls, this hasn't been dealt with in this section in detail. However, you can find the complete coding in Listing 7.10. You can check the complete flow logic on the dynpro in Listing 7.11.

```
*&--------------------------------------------------------------*
*&      Module  TC_MRM_CUST_CHANGE_FIELD_ATTR   OUTPUT
*&--------------------------------------------------------------*
MODULE tc_mrm_cust_change_field_attr OUTPUT.
  DATA ls_col TYPE cxtab_column.

* For all columns of the current line
  LOOP AT tc_mrm_cust-cols INTO ls_col.

* Standard fields: Prevent input
    IF ls_col-screen-name EQ 'GS_DRSEG_CI-C_RBLGP' OR
       ls_col-screen-name EQ 'GS_DRSEG_CI-C_KOART' OR
       ls_col-screen-name EQ 'GS_DRSEG_CI-C_MATNR'.
      ls_col-screen-input = 0.
    ENDIF.

* In display mode or if no item number
* is assigned – prevent input for custom fields
    IF ls_col-screen-name EQ 'GS_DRSEG_CI-ZZTEXT_1' OR
       ls_col-screen-name EQ 'GS_DRSEG_CI-ZZTEXT_2'.
      IF gv_trtyp = 'A' OR
         gs_drseg_ci-c_rblgp IS INITIAL.
        ls_col-screen-input = 0.
      ELSE.
        ls_col-screen-input = 1.
      ENDIF.
    ENDIF.

    MODIFY tc_mrm_cust-cols FROM ls_col.
  ENDLOOP.

ENDMODULE.              " TC_MRM_CUST_CHANGE_FIELD_ATTR  OUTPUT
```

Listing 7.10 Module TC_MRM_CUST_GET_LINES OUTPUT

```
PROCESS BEFORE OUTPUT.
  MODULE get_data.

*&SPWIZARD: PBO FLOW LOGIC FOR TABLECONTROL 'TC_MRM_CUST'
  MODULE tc_mrm_cust_change_tc_attr.
*&SPWIZARD: MODULE TC_MRM_CUST_CHANGE_COL_ATTR.
  LOOP AT   gt_drseg_ci
       INTO gs_drseg_ci
       WITH CONTROL tc_mrm_cust
       CURSOR tc_mrm_cust-current_line.
    MODULE tc_mrm_cust_get_lines.
    MODULE tc_mrm_cust_change_field_attr.
  ENDLOOP.

PROCESS AFTER INPUT.
*&SPWIZARD: PAI FLOW LOGIC FOR TABLECONTROL 'TC_MRM_CUST'
  LOOP AT gt_drseg_ci.
    CHAIN.
      FIELD gs_drseg_ci-c_rblgp.
      FIELD gs_drseg_ci-c_koart.
      FIELD gs_drseg_ci-c_matnr.
      FIELD gs_drseg_ci-zztext_1.
      FIELD gs_drseg_ci-zztext_2.
      MODULE tc_mrm_cust_modify ON CHAIN-REQUEST.
    ENDCHAIN.
  ENDLOOP.

  MODULE tc_mrm_cust_user_command.

  MODULE write_data.
```
Listing 7.11 Flow Logic on Dynpro 0100

7.2   Overriding Tolerance Checks

Many options are provided with the tolerance limits in the Customizing of Logistics Invoice Verification to influence the locking procedure of incoming invoices with regard to price or quantity variances. When the incoming invoice is entered, the absolute or percent upper and lower limits are checked. If a value (quantity/price) deviates beyond these limits from the associated purchase order, the document is locked. As a result of the locking, the invoice cannot be cleared in FI until the lock has been removed. With the enhancement `MM08R002`, you can also individually override these upper and lower limits.

7.2.1 Tolerance Limits in Customizing

In Customizing (Transaction SPRO), you can find the settings for tolerance limits under MATERIALS MANAGEMENT • LOGISTICS INVOICE VERIFICATION • INVOICE LOCK • SPECIFY TOLERANCE LIMITS. Depending on the company code and the tolerance key, you can maintain the absolute and percent upper limits and lower limits for differences here (see Figure 7.8).

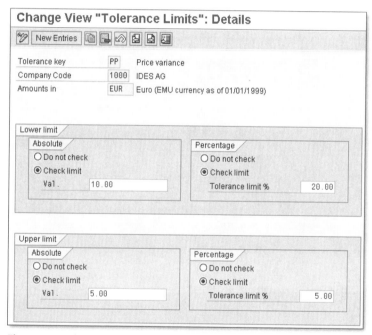

Figure 7.8 Tolerance Limits in Customizing

If you set the DO NOT CHECK option with a limit, the invoice item may differ indefinitely in this direction. If these limits are exceeded, the invoice can be saved (in the standard version, the associated message is set as a warning); however, it is supplied with a locking reason.

The tolerance key stands for an SAP-specified type of deviation between the incoming invoice and purchase order or the goods receipt (GR). You can see in Table 7.6

a brief overview of all the tolerance keys checked by the system. You can also find detailed descriptions on the individual keys in the Customizing documentation.

Tolerance Key	Explanation
AN	Amount of item without purchase order reference
AP	Amount of item with purchase order reference
BD	Write off small differences automatically
BR	Percentage purchase order price quantity variance (IR prior to GR)
BW	Percentage purchase order price quantity variance (IR following GR)
DQ	Exceed amount: Quantity variance
DW	Quantity variance when GR quantity = zero
KW	Price variance: Delivery costs
LA	Amount of blanket purchase order
LD	Blanket purchase or time limit exceeded
PP	Price variance
PS	Price variance: Estimated price
ST	Date variance
VP	Moving average price variance

Table 7.6 Overview of Tolerance Key

7.2.2 Use of the Enhancement

Enhancement MM08R002 is also described using a brief example. Let's assume that you have set the tolerance limits for price variances on the purchase order (tolerance key PP) in such a way that only 2 percent variance in either direction is allowed. You now have a material group where the prices for the goods are subject to significant market fluctuations. Therefore, a variance of 5 percent is allowed in this case. To implement this, you need to know which material group the material of an invoice item belongs to; depending on this information, you must then redefine the limits. Unfortunately, you receive this information in a different user exit from the one used to overwrite parameters.

Take a look at Table 7.7. When you enter an item in the incoming invoice and there is a variance, the EXIT_SAPLMR1M_001 or EXIT_SAPLMRMP_001 is called depending on the type of variance. You must copy the header and item data to the global data of the function group. Then the EXIT_SAPLMRMC_001 starts in which you can redefine the tolerance limits. You can access the header and item data again via the global data of the function group.

User Exit	Description
EXIT_SAPLMR1M_001	Price and quantity variances are run for each item and contain header and item data of the item.
EXIT_SAPLMRMP_001	Date and amount variances are run for each item and contain header and item data of the item.
EXIT_SAPLMRMC_001	Each item and relevant tolerance key is run and provides the option to redefine the tolerance limits.

Table 7.7 User Exits of the Enhancement MM08R002

The following instructions put the theory into practice:

1. Create a new project in Transaction CMOD, and include the enhancement MM08R002. Then save the project, and switch to COMPONENTS.

2. Navigate to EXIT_SAPLMR1M_001, and choose the SKIP • GLOBAL DATA menu option. You cannot directly change the global data of a user exit because that's a modification. You can, however, find a line in the global date with the content INCLUDE ZXM08TOP. This include is in the customer namespace, and you can customize it without any modifications.

   Double-click the name of the include to create this. Then define two structures to include the header and item data from the interface of the exit. You can copy the data types from the interface of the user exit (see Listing 7.12).

```
*&---------------------------------------------------------------------*
*&  Include           ZXM08TOP
*&---------------------------------------------------------------------*

* Global Data: header and item data
DATA: zz_rbkpv TYPE MRM_RBKPV,
      zz_drseg TYPE MMCR_DRSEG.
```

Listing 7.12 Global Data of the Enhancement

3. Navigate back to the user exit, and double-click to create the include ZXM08U04. Transfer the data from the interface to the global structures just defined (see Listing 7.13).

```
*&---------------------------------------------------------*
*&  Include          ZXM08U04 (EXIT_SAPLMR1M_001)
*&---------------------------------------------------------*
*"*"Local interface:
*"  IMPORTING
*"     VALUE(I_RBKPV) TYPE   MRM_RBKPV
*"     VALUE(I_YDRSEG) TYPE   MMCR_DRSEG
*"  EXCEPTIONS
*"       CALL_FAILURE
*"---------------------------------------------------------
zz_rbkpv = i_rbkpv.
zz_drseg = i_ydrseg.
```

Listing 7.13 User Exit EXIT_SAPLMR1M_001

4. Switch to the user exit EXIT_SAPLMRMP_001, and create the include ZXM08U17. Transfer the data of the interface here to the global data. The coding is identical with Listing 7.13.

5. Navigate to EXIT_SAPLMRMC_001, and create the include ZXM08U19. Two import parameters are provided in this user exit: The company code and the tolerance key. You should therefore redefine the limits based on these parameters.

The new tolerance limits can be specified using Table 7.8. The fields E_XW1JA, E_XW2JA, E_XP1JA, and E_XP2JA specify whether the associated limited is checked, identically with DO NOT CHECK and CHECK LIMIT in Customizing (see Figure 7.8). When you don't set the flag, an unrestricted variance is allowed here.

Parameter	Explanation
E_WERT1	Lower limit absolute
E_XW1JA	Check lower limit absolutely
E_WERT2	Upper limit absolute
E_XW2JA	Check lower limit absolutely

Table 7.8 Parameter of the EXIT_SAPLMRMC_001

Parameter	Explanation
E_PROZ1	Lower limit in percentage terms
E_XP1JA	Check lower limit in percentage terms
E_PROZ2	Upper limit in percentage terms
E_XP2JA	Check upper limit in percentage terms
E_CHECK	Characteristic: Use new limits from user exit

Table 7.8 Parameter of the EXIT_SAPLMRMC_001 (Cont.)

6. Place the flag E_CHECK to apply your changes; otherwise, the settings will continue to be used from Customizing.

> **Note**
>
> If you set E_CHECK and don't fill any field, this basically means that unlimited variances are allowed. Because only the percentage limit in the given example is customized, you can optionally read all other values from Customizing (Table T169G). You can find an example for this in Listing 7.14.

```
*&--------------------------------------------------------------*
*&  Include           ZXM08U19 (EXIT_SAPLMRMC_001)
*&--------------------------------------------------------------*
DATA ls_t169g TYPE t169g.

* Differing logic for all company codes
* and price variance (tolerance key PP)
* for material group 007
IF i_tolsl = 'PP' AND
   zz_drseg-matkl = '007'.
* Obtain standard values from Customizing
  SELECT SINGLE * FROM t169g INTO ls_t169g
       WHERE bukrs = i_bukrs AND
             tolsl = i_tolsl.
* Assign absolute limits from Customizing
  e_wert1 = ls_t169g-wert1.
  e_wert2 = ls_t169g-wert2.
  e_xw1ja = ls_t169g-xw1ja.
  e_xw2ja = ls_t169g-xw2ja.
```

```
* Increase percentage variance
  e_proz1 = 5.
  e_xp1ja = 'X'.
  e_proz2 = 5.
  e_xp2ja = 'X'.
* Use change
  e_check = 'X'.
ENDIF.
```

Listing 7.14 User Exit EXIT_SAPLMRMC_001

8 Validation and Substitution of Accounting Documents

Perhaps you are wondering why there is a chapter on validation and substitution in SAP ERP Financials (FI) in a book about MM enhancements. The easy answer is that numerous MM documents have an FI document as a follow-on. Therefore, you often need to check information from an MM document from the FI point of view and reject the booking if necessary. Information from MM documents is frequently formatted and copied to fields of the FI document. The item text (BSEG-SGTXT) and reference key (BSEG-XREF1/2) fields are very popular here in particular. Both can be neatly resolved via validation and substitution.

Validation and Substitution

With validation and substitution, you have two very similar tools provided. The difference between the two is as follows:

► **Validation**
With validation, you can check the field contents of the accounting document and prevent the posting of a document if required by displaying an error message.

► **Substitution**
With substitution, you can overwrite some field contents of the accounting document.

Of course, you also have the option in many MM transactions to check an input or overwrite field contents via suitable user exits or BAdIs. However, the advantage of validation and substitution is that there is a central item in the interface between MM and FI. Therefore, you can implement a central set of rules in validation that will always run regardless of whether the original document is a material document, a logistics incoming invoice, or a document from another application, such as from Sales and Distribution (SD) or FI.

In the following sections, you'll learn about the function of validation and substitution based on an example.

8.1   Validation of Accounting Documents

You can use validation to check an accounting document and to reject the posting, if applicable. You create a validation in Transaction OB28. A validation for a specific callup point is therefore created and contains one or several steps. Each step in turn consists of a prerequisite, a check, and a message displayed if the check fails (see Figure 8.1). You should learn a lot more about the concept before you create an initial validation, and we will provide this additional information in the following subsections.

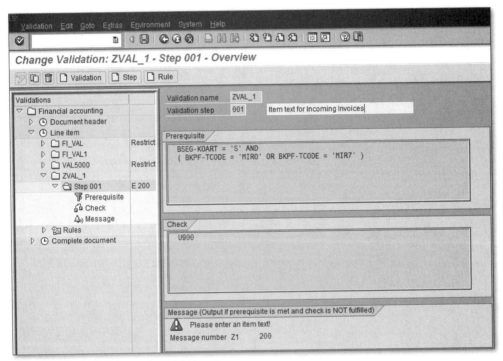

Figure 8.1 Overview of a Validation Step

8.1.1   Callup Points

Validation can be triggered at various callup points; usually this happens during the check for the document header or the document item takes place. This always refers to the FI document itself and not to the data of the original document, which can originate from many areas. The header data consists of the fields of Table BKPF. The item data consists of the fields of Table BSEG.

A Boolean class is defined behind each callup point. The Boolean class controls the tables and fields as well as the message class that is used for error messages. An overview of the possible modules is provided in Table 8.1.

Callup point	Boolean class	Scope of check
0001	008	Document header (BKPF)
0002	009	Document item (BSEG)
0003	015	Total document (BKPF and BSEG)

Table 8.1 Callup Points in the Validation and Substitution

8.1.2 Steps

Each validation consists of one or several steps that are executed in succession. Each step consists of the following sections:

▶ **Prerequisites**
In the PREREQUISITE section, you establish whether this step is required for the current document and whether it will be executed. A typical query is, for example, the transaction code according to this (BKPF-TCODE) to check the origin of the document as well as all fields from the document header (Callup points 1 and 2), and the document items (Callup point 2).

▶ **Check**
In the CHECK section, you specify a condition that must be fulfilled to run the program without errors and therefore to post the document. You can check all fields for specific contents or constants, and you can link several field checks if required.

You can also go to a validation exit for complex checks and carry out the checks via a normal ABAP coding. To do this, you need to return the result of your checks to the variable B_RESULT (FALSE or TRUE).

▶ **Message**
In the MESSAGE section, you ultimately define the message displayed to the user if the previously defined check has failed. For documents from MM, the message is passed on so that it appears within the MM application if the FI document cannot be posted because of checks. When you create the initial validation for a Boolean class, you are asked for a message class that applies to all messages in this area in the future.

> **Change to Message Class**
>
> When you create the validation for a Boolean class, the message class is specified. This assignment is permanently stored from this time on and cannot be undone when an existing validation has been deleted. If this assignment is changed, use Report RGUGBR28 (see SAP Note 6975). Then start Program RGUGBR00 (without the last two options) to regenerate the validations substitutions and rules.

8.1.3 Example without Exit Routine

Now that you understand the basic concepts for validation, the following brief example shows you how to set up a validation. Of course, your actual checks will be considerably more comprehensive. However, we're only describing the underlying concept at this point.

Let's assume that your financial accounting department wants to have a specific classification key for evaluations in the field item text (BSEG-SGTXT). The assignment key might, for example, display an area of your enterprise so that it can be displayed quickly in lists on open items. You should make sure that this field is entered correctly in Logistics Invoice Verification. The item text is copied automatically from the respective text field (DRSEG-SGTXT) of the incoming invoice. However, check to make sure a text is entered here. The classification keys that are predefined by financial accounting all start with OS. Therefore, check whether this text is at the first two positions of the entered text.

1. Start Transaction OB28. In the initial screen (see Figure 8.2), you can create a validation for each company code and time. In the example, a check of the document items is executed, that is, for Callup point 2. If, in your case, a validation already exists for this callup point, you can navigate to this point by double-clicking the validation. If not, enter any name for the validation, and then double-click the name. Confirm in the dialog that you now want to create this validation.

2. In the validation editor (refer to Figure 8.1), check whether your validation is highlighted in the callup point document item in the left-hand navigation bar. Then click the STEP icon ([Ctrl] + [Shift] + [F5]) to insert a new step.

3. Give the step a name, for example, "SGTXT: Check classification key", and switch to the PREREQUISITE section.

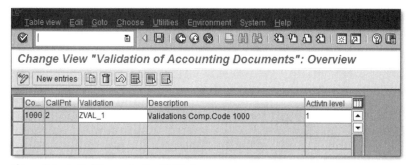

Figure 8.2   Initial Screen to the Validation

4. You can carry out the prerequisites by choosing the fields from the LIST OF THE STRUCTURES by double-clicking and inserting comparisons on the operators on the right-hand side. If you choose this variant, you can change the view via menu path SETTINGS • TECHNICAL NAME so that you can see the technical field names. Switch back again to the standard view via menu path SETTINGS • SHORT DESCRIPTIONS.

For experienced users, you can switch to a mode via SETTINGS • EXPERT MODE, which allows the direct input of conditions. You can now perform this change at least for this example.

5. The check only runs if the document originates from the Logistic Invoice Verification (Transaction MIRO) or the parked document (Transaction MIR7). Also, the text is only copied into GL account lines, not into the vendor line. For this reason, the check may only take place when the account type (BSEG-KOART) is 'S' for GL account. Enter the prerequisite as shown in Listing 8.1.

```
BSEG-KOART = 'S' AND
( BKPF-TCODE = 'MIRO' OR BKPF-TCODE = 'MIR7' )
```

Listing 8.1 Prerequisite for the Validation

6. Now switch to the CHECK section. The GL account lines must have an item text that starts with OS. For this, you can simply use the asterisk as the usual placeholder. However, you need the keyword LIKE as a relational operator. Enter the following line as a check:

```
BSEG-SGTXT LIKE 'OS*'
```

7. A message is displayed if the previous check fails. You maintain these in the section MESSAGE, to which you now navigate to. At this point, you can view the message class in which the messages for the validation are stored. You can

navigate directly to the maintenance of messages via the pencil icon on the right-hand side of the message class. Highlight a free message number, and click INDIVIDUAL MAINTENANCE.

8. Enter the text for the message, for example, "Please enter a sort key!" Save the change, and navigate via BACK ([F3]) again to the CHECK section. You can also perform the message maintenance directly in Transaction SE91.

9. Enter the message number in the respective field of the validation. Leave the message type as an error message. You can only display warning messages when required. The additional transfer of message variables with additional information is possible here.

10. Click again on your step in the left-hand bar, and save your changes. The step should now appear as in Figure 8.3.

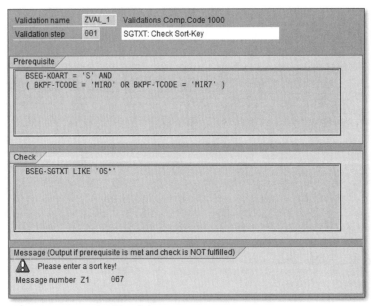

Figure 8.3 Example of a Validation

11. You must still activate the validation so that it will actually run. Switch back to the initial screen of the validation (Transaction OB28). When you've created the validation, the right-hand column DEGREE OF ACTIVATION is still empty. In this case, the validation is not executed. Change the degree of activation to 1

to fundamentally run the validation. With the degree of activation 2, the validation is activated but is bypassed for batch input.

12. As an example, if you now enter an incoming invoice with a purchase order reference with Transaction MIRO, you must enter a text for each item starting with 0S; otherwise, you receive an error message.

8.1.4   Example with Exit Routine

For simple checks, the variant already mentioned in Section 8.1.3, Example without Exit Routine, is sufficient. Let's now assume that you want to enhance the check from the previous example so that only classification keys can still be used that have been defined in a custom table. This means that you must execute a database query. This is only possible via an exit routine. To use exit routines, you must first recall some basics.

Exit routines for validation or substitution are form routines that are stored in a specific program. The program is maintained in the Customizing Table T80D (see Figure 8.4). One program is stored here for each work area (type `Module pool`) that includes exit routines. The work area is relevant for the validation GBLR. The program RGGBR000 is stored here in the standard. If you want to store custom form routines, you must copy the program RGGBR000, for example, to ZGGBR000, and change the entry accordingly in Table T80D.

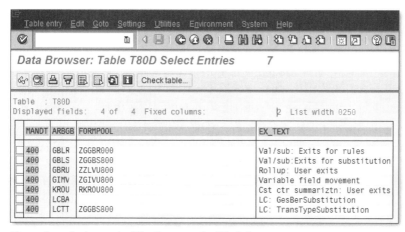

Figure 8.4 Assignment of the Programs for Work Areas

You implement the example by using an exit routine with the following steps:

1. If nothing has happened yet in your system, copy the program RGGBR000 to your namespace, and change the entry for the work area GBLR in Table T80D.

2. Two steps are necessary to enhance the program with a new exit routine. First, the new routine must be created. User routines should always start with U, and use a three-digit number. The basic framework for such a routine is shown in Listing 8.2.

```
*-------------------------------------------------------------
*       Validation Exit
*-------------------------------------------------------------*
*   <-B_RESULT    T = True   F = False                        *
*-------------------------------------------------------------*
FORM u900 USING b_result.

ENDFORM.
```

Listing 8.2 Standard Framework for Exit Routines in the Validation

3. Next, this exit routine must be announced to the validation. For this, there is a predefined form called get_exit_titles. in the program ZGGBR000. This form returns an internal Table ETAB with all defined form routines. This table is filled from the uniform internal Table EXITS. You can fill these as follows:

```
exits-name  = 'U900'.
exits-param = c_exit_param_none.
exits-title = text-900.
APPEND exits.
```

You fill the field NAME with the name of the form routine; the field TITLE contains a descriptive text. If you use a text element (TEXT-###) for this, this text can be created in several languages. You ultimately fill the field PARAM with one of the three possible variants of the interface for the form routine. You can always work with the constant for the validation C_EXIT_PARAM_NONE (see Table 8.2).

4. Edit your previously defined program. Create a new, still empty form routine, as described earlier. Enhance the form get_exit_titles to return the name of your new form.

Parameter Type/Constant	Description
C_EXIT_PARAM_NONE	The form routine (besides B_RESULT) does not contain any other parameters.
C_EXIT_PARAM_FIELD	The form routine uses an additional field that is to be changed (in substitution).
C_EXIT_PARAM_CLASS	All data is handled as a parameter. This exit type can only be used in matrix validations or substitutions.

Table 8.2 Parameter Types for Exit Routines

5. The check is executed using a database table. For this, create a table in the ABAP Dictionary (Transaction SE11). You can view a simple example of this in Figure 8.5. Next, maintain the table, and create some entries that start with OS.

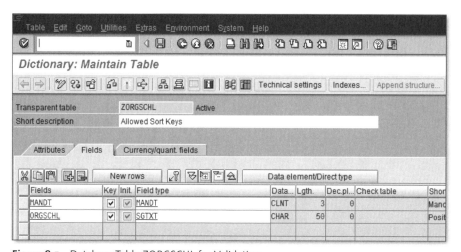

Figure 8.5 Database Table ZORGSCHL for Validation

6. Now you can program the new exit routine. Check whether the content of the entered item text (BSEG-SGTXT) in the previously defined table has been entered. If this is the case, set B_RESULT to True (T); if not, set it to False (F). To access BSEG, you need to announce this structure via a TABLES command. You can find some commented lines on this at the beginning of the report, which you can simply activate.

Although a document contains several items, you must view the exit BSEG as a structure. The exit is called several times when the document is updated, once for each item. BSEG contains the respective item in each case. In Listing 8.3, you can find a complete program with the new exit routine taken from the example.

```
PROGRAM zggbr000.

INCLUDE fgbbgd00.                "Data types

*!!!!!!!!!!!!!!!!!!!!!!!!!!!!!!!!!!!!!!!!!!!!!!!!!!!!!!!!!!!!!!!!*
* PLEASE INCLUDE THE FOLLOWING "TYPE-POOL" AND "TABLES"
* COMMANDS IF THE ACCOUNTING MODULE IS INSTALLED IN
* YOUR SYSTEM
TYPE-POOLS: GB002. " TO BE INCLUDED IN
TABLES: BKPF,      " ANY SYSTEM THAT
        BSEG,      " HAS 'FI' INSTALLED
        COBL,
        GLU1.
*!!!!!!!!!!!!!!!!!!!!!!!!!!!!!!!!!!!!!!!!!!!!!!!!!!!!!!!!!!!!!!!!*


*--------------------------------------------------------------*
*       FORM GET_EXIT_TITLES                                   *
*--------------------------------------------------------------*
FORM get_exit_titles TABLES etab.

  DATA: BEGIN OF exits OCCURS 50,
          name(5)    TYPE c,
          param      LIKE c_exit_param_none,
          title(60) TYPE c,
        END OF exits.

  exits-name  = 'U900'.
  exits-param = c_exit_param_none.
  exits-title = text-900.
  APPEND exits.

  REFRESH etab.
  LOOP AT exits.
    etab = exits.
    APPEND etab.
```

```
    ENDLOOP.

ENDFORM.                        "GET_EXIT_TITLES


*------------------------------------------------------------------
*         Validation Exit
*-----------------------------------------------------------------*
*   <--  B_RESULT    T = True  F = False                          *
*-----------------------------------------------------------------*
FORM u900 USING b_result.
  DATA ls_zorgschl TYPE zorgschl.

  SELECT SINGLE * FROM zorgschl INTO ls_zorgschl
                 WHERE orgschl = bseg-sgtxt.
  IF sy-subrc = 0.
    b_result = 'T'.
  ELSE.
    b_result = 'F'.
  ENDIF.
ENDFORM.
```

Listing 8.3 Exit Form Pool for the Validation (Extract from the Program ZGGBR000)

7. Restart Transaction OB28 if applicable. Otherwise, the new exit routine is still unknown. Switch to the validation and to the step that you created in Section 8.1.3, Example without Exit Routine. Then click CHECK to switch there.

8. Switch again to the expert mode, and delete the checks created in the previous example. Now simply write the name of the exit routine, for example, U900, in the formula editor. Alternatively, you can switch to the EXITS tabstrip, and copy the routine U900 by double-clicking.

9. Now test the entry of an incoming invoice again via Transaction MIRO. You must now store a text in the items that is created in Table ZORGSCHL; otherwise, you receive the defined error message.

Tip

You may use exit routines both in validation and in substitution as a prerequisite. You therefore have a very flexible option to control the execution of a step. Here, you work again with the return value B_RESULT that you fill either with T (True, the prerequisite is fulfilled) or F (False, the prerequisite is not fulfilled).

8.2 Substitution of Accounting Documents

Substitution allows the replacement of some fields of the accounting document during its posting. Substitution is in many respects very similar to validation. For this reason, you should definitely take a look at Section 8.1, Validation of Accounting Documents, because not all of the basics are repeated here. You should already understand the concept of times and steps, in particular (see Section 8.1.1, Callup Point, and 8.1.2, Steps).

You access the substitution via Transaction OBBH. With the validation, you can create a substitution for each company code and callup point. Each substitution is divided into steps that are processed in sequence. The steps themselves in turn consist of a prerequisite and the substitution itself. You can no longer display error messages here. Substitution doesn't include a MESSAGES section (see Figure 8.6).

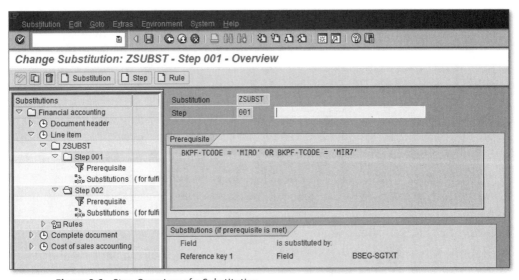

Figure 8.6 Step Overview of a Substitution

Which Fields Are Available in Substitution?

The interchangeable fields can be controlled via Table GB01. All fields from the document header and document item can be substituted; that is, they can be overwritten with new values, which are assigned in Table GB01 of the Boolean class (refer to Table 8.1), and haven't been explicitly excluded from this via the field BEXCLUDE.

You can display the content of the table with the following selection parameters:

- BOOLCLASS
  008 for document header (Callup point 1) or 009 for document item (Callup point 2). Callup point 3 (Boolean class 015) no longer plays any role in substitution because no fields are allowed here.
- CLASSTYPE
  S (Substitution).
- BCLTAB
  BKPF for document header or BSEG for document item.

All listed fields (the field name is in BCLFIELD) may be substituted, if the indicator BEX-CLUDE is not set. Furthermore, for Callup point 2 it is allowed to release additional fields by customizing Table GB01. The additional fields are listed here:

- BSEG-FIPOS (financing item)
- BSEG-HBKID (short key for a house bank)
- BSEG-MSCHL (dunning key)
- BSEG-MANSP (dunning block indicator)
- BSEG-MADAT (date of the last reminder notice)
- BSEG-MANST (dunning level)
- BSEG-MABER (dunning area)
- BSEG-RSTGR (reason code for payments)
- BSEG-ZLSPR (key for payment blocking indicator)

After you've customized the table, you must start Report RGUGBR00 to regenerate the programs for the substitution. Before you customize Table GB01, refer also to SAP Note 42615 for more detailed information on this.

You can execute the substitution itself via a simple formula assignment or a substitution exit. The following subsection is a simple example again for both variants that describes the principle of substitution.

8.2.1   Substitution without Exit Routine

Let's assume that you want to replace the field BSEG-XREF1 (reference key) with a new value. You have two options for this without replacing an exit routine: You can either copy the field content from another field or overwrite the field content with a constant value.

1. Start Transaction OBBH. Because the field BSEG-XREF1 belongs to the items of the FI document, you must use a substitution for the Callup point 2. Create a substitution for a company code on the Callup point 2 by providing any name

and double-clicking the substitution. Alternatively, navigate to an already-existing substitution by double-clicking.

2. In the tree structure on the left-hand side, the chosen substitution should now be automatically selected. If not, click your substitution to highlight it. Click STEP to create a new step within the substitution.

3. A dialog window appears that maps all interchangeable fields at this point. You can now select one or several of the fields. The field BSEG-XREF1 is adequate for the example. Then confirm the dialog by pressing the [Enter] key.

4. Another dialog window now appears for each previously chosen field and offers three selection options:

   ▶ CONSTANT VALUE
   You can replace the field with a constant, that is, with any definable text.

   ▶ EXIT
   You can choose an exit routine and replace the field with ABAP coding.

   ▶ FIELD – FIELD ASSIGNMENT
   You can overwrite the content of the field with the content from another field of the document.

   Choose the FIELD – FIELD ASSIGNMENT option, and confirm the dialog by pressing the [Enter] key.

5. Identify the step with a descriptive text, and go to the PREREQUISITE section. Switch to the expert mode (SETTINGS • EXPERT MODE), and enter the following condition to only implement the substitution when the document originates from Logistics Invoice Verification:

   ```
   BKPF-TCODE = 'MIRO' OR BKPF-TCODE = 'MIR7'
   ```

6. Edit the SUBSTITUTION section. For each field that you have selected in the dialog window (that has appeared when you created a new step), you can now specify the source of the substitution. The field REFERENCE KEY 1 (XREF1) will be overwritten by the content of BSEG-SGTXT, which means you enter this field as a source on the right-hand side (see Figure 8.7). You receive a warning message that the field XREF1 is shorter than SGTXT and that may therefore be lost — only the first 12 characters from SGTXT are copied.

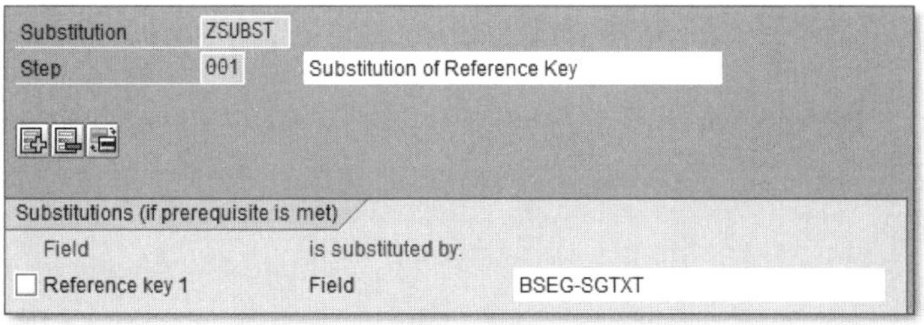

Figure 8.7 Field-Field Assignment in the Substitution

7. You must still activate the substitution so that it will run. To do this, switch again to the initial screen of the substitution (Transaction OBBH). When you have created the substitution, the right-hand column DEGREE OF ACTIVATION is still empty. In this case, the substitution is not executed. Change the degree of activation to 1 to run the substitution. With the degree of activation 2, the substitution is activated but is bypassed with batch input.

8.2.2 Substitution with Exit Routine

Simple substitution without using ABAP coding quickly reaches its limits. However, just as with validation, it is possible to enhance a form routine pool with custom routines and to run these in the substitution when required. You can find some basics on using exit routines in the validation described in more detail in Section 8.1.4, Example with Exit Routine.

The program containing the available form routines is maintained for substitution in Table T80D (see Figure 8.4). The program on the work area GBLS must be maintained for substitution. Program RGGBS000 is stored here by default. To add custom routines, you must copy the program into the custom namespace and change the entry accordingly in T80D.

1. If this has not yet happened in your system, copy Program RGGBS000 into your namespace, and change the entry for the work area GBLS in Table T80D.

2. You must also define form routines in substitution by including them in the internal Table ETAB (via Table EXITS) in the form get_exit_titles. You define the interface so that a field can be transferred as a parameter (the field that is later substituted). For this, set the field PARAM to C_EXIT_PARAM_FIELD (refer to Table 8.2):

```
exits-name  = 'U900'.
exits-param = c_exit_param_field.
```

```
exits-title = text-900.
APPEND exits.
```

It's then specified that the form routine U900 contains a field in the parameter interface. The field must not have a type and can also have any name in the interface. You define which field with which type is actually transferred later in Transaction OBBH. The field is then substituted by a simple assignment of a value.

You must, however, make sure that you don't cause any type conflict with regard to the assignment that would then only show for the runtime. The standard framework for a substitution routine is given in Listing 8.4.

```
*---------------------------------------------------------------
*        Substitution Exit
*---------------------------------------------------------------*
FORM u900 USING ref_key.
*  Substitution is carried out by assignment
*  ref_key = ...
ENDFORM.
```

Listing 8.4 Standard Framework for Exit Routines in the Substitution

If, for example, the field reference key 2 (BSEG-XREF2) is filled with a combination of the reference activity and posting user, the complete example would appear as in Listing 8.5. Here, you can also read data from custom tables to implement more complex populations of the field.

3. Modify your previously changed program, and insert a custom routine to substitute the field BSEG-XREF2. Register this routine in the form get_exit_titles, and use the parameter C_EXIT_PARAM_FIELD. You can use Listing 8.5 as a sample.

```
PROGRAM zggbs000.
INCLUDE fgbbgd00.              "Standard data types

*!!!!!!!!!!!!!!!!!!!!!!!!!!!!!!!!!!!!!!!!!!!!!!!!!!!!!!!!!!!!!!!!!*
* PLEASE INCLUDE THE FOLLOWING "TYPE-POOL" AND "TABLES"
* COMMANDS IF THE ACCOUNTING MODULE IS INSTALLED IN
* YOUR SYSTEM
TYPE-POOLS: GB002. " TO BE INCLUDED IN
TABLES: BKPF,      " ANY SYSTEM THAT
        BSEG,      " HAS 'FI' INSTALLED
        COBL,
```

```
        CSKS,
        ANLZ,
        GLU1.
*!!!!!!!!!!!!!!!!!!!!!!!!!!!!!!!!!!!!!!!!!!!!!!!!!!!!!!!!!!!!!!!!*

*--------------------------------------------------------------*
*        FORM GET_EXIT_TITLES
*--------------------------------------------------------------*
FORM get_exit_titles TABLES etab.
  DATA: begin of exits occurs 50,
          name(5)   type c,
          param     like c_exit_param_none,
          title(60) type c,
        end of exits.

* Register exit U900
  exits-name  = 'U900'.
  exits-param = c_exit_param_field.
  exits-title = text-900.
  APPEND exits.

  REFRESH etab.
  LOOP AT exits.
    etab = exits.
    APPEND etab.
  ENDLOOP.
ENDFORM.


*--------------------------------------------------------------*
*        FORM U900
*--------------------------------------------------------------*
FORM u900 USING ref_key.
  DATA lv_xref2 TYPE bseg-xref2.

* XREF2 has only twelve characters, concatenate BKPF-AWTYP 5, BKPF-
USNAM 12
* suitably:
  CONCATENATE bkpf-awtyp(4) bkpf-usnam(8) INTO lv_xref2.

*  Substitution is carried out by assignment
  ref_key = lv_xref2.
ENDFORM.
```

Listing 8.5 User Exit Form Pool for Substitution

187

4. Start Transaction OBBH, and select your already available substitution on Callup point 2. Generate a new STEP, choose the field BSEG-XREF2 in the dialog window, and confirm the dialog by pressing the Enter key.

5. In the next dialog window, select the EXIT option as the source for the substitution. Confirm this dialog also via the Enter key.

6. Then switch to the PREREQUISITE section. Here you can again use the following condition:

```
BKPF-TCODE = 'MIRO' OR BKPF-TCODE = 'MIR7'
```

7. In the SUBSTITUTIONS section, you can now assign the previously defined exit (see Figure 8.8).

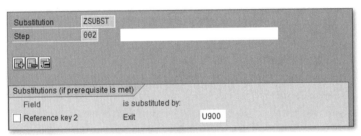

Figure 8.8 Substitution with Exit Routine

8. Save your changes, and check that your substitution is active in the initial screen of Transaction OBBH. If you now post a logistics invoice, the content of the field BSEG-XREF1 is overwritten according to the coding.

8.2.3 Read Access to Data of the Source Document

You usually only have access to fields of the FI document in substitution. You may possibly want to format the fields from the original document, which has not been copied into the FI document to therefore substitute another field in the FI document. This could be particularly interesting if you use custom fields in the original document, which you want to copy into a field of the FI document without too much effort. You would, for example, have the option of creating a new input field in Logistics Invoice Verification, the content of which is copied into the field XREF1 of the FI document. Normally, you can directly maintain only the item text (SGTXT) in Logistics Invoice Verification.

Using a small trick, you can gain access to this data in individual cases: The posting of the FI document and substitution is called from the original document. From the program point of view, other programs or function modules are called from the original program. You can look at the exact call stack in the debugger when you place a breakpoint in the substitutions exit, post a document, and then switch to the respective view in the debugger. In Figure 8.9, you can see this view for a logistics invoice (MIRO/MIR7) in the classic debugger.

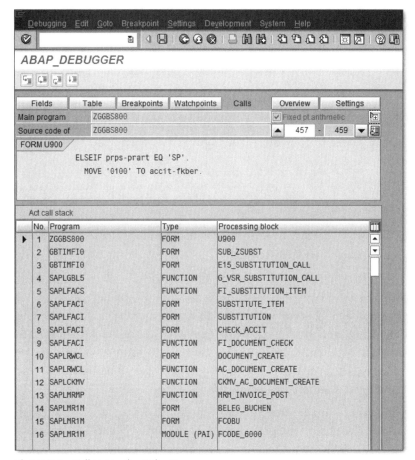

Figure 8.9 Call List in the Debugger

As you can see from this view, the original program name (in which the form BELEG_BUCHEN will run) is SAPLMR1M. By double-clicking the call stack, you can navigate to the respective level and search for data objects in the codes that are available there. Finding the appropriate data can sometimes be difficult. Moreover, you must ensure that this data object is defined in the global area of the program (you do not have any access to local variables). There are items in the internal table YDRSEG for the logistics invoice.

You can check whether external access to a data object is possible by switching again (with a double-click) to the top level of the call stack in the debugger and trying to display the variable there. The entry is made in the sample (PROGRAMMNAME) VARIABLE, for example, (SAPLMR1M)YDRSEG. Is the content displayed to you in the debugger? Congratulations! You can now also access it in substitution.

1. You cannot directly access the variable (SAPLMR1M)YDRSEG. This is unknown in the form pool of substitution, and you receive a syntax error. Instead, you must first create a constant of the ABAP type C (Character), and then assign the variable name. If it is an internal table as described in the example given, you should explicitly refer to the content of the internal table (and not, for instance, to the possibly available header line). You execute this by attaching square brackets:

   (SAPLMR1M)YDRSEG[].

2. Define a field symbol, and assign the content to the constant. Write the name of the constant in brackets; otherwise, you would be able to see the constant itself via the field symbol. The command for this is the following:

   ASSIGN (c_constant) TO <fieldsymbol>.

   The field symbol now displays for you the content of the internal table YDRSEG.

3. Create an internal table identical to Table YDRSEG, and copy the content into your custom table. Only work with your local copy, and do not touch the original. Each unintentional change to the original data could have disastrous consequences and result in inconsistencies. As long as you use the data only for read access in the copy, then there is no danger.

4. If you haven't already linked substitution as a result of the prerequisite to a specific transaction, you should integrate a check on sy-tcode by now, at the latest, in the program. Bear in mind that the program variable(SAPLMR1M)YDRSEG is only available when the original document is a logistics invoice.

Listing 8.6 shows a customized variant of the form U900. There is a custom field named ZZ_FELD at the item level in the logistics invoice be copied to BSEG-XREF1.

```
*-------------------------------------------------------------
*        Substitution Exit U900
*-------------------------------------------------------------*
```

```
FORM u900 USING ref_key.

* Define constant and field symbol
  CONSTANTS c_drseg(18) TYPE c VALUE '(SAPLMR1M)YDRSEG[]'.
  FIELD-SYMBOLS <ydrseg> TYPE ANY TABLE.

* Type-Pool MMCR contains the necessary data type for
* the local copy of the YDRSEG
  TYPE-POOLS mmcr.
  DATA gt_ydrseg TYPE TABLE OF mmcr_drseg.
  DATA gs_ydrseg TYPE mmcr_drseg.

* Execution only when the posting comes from the logistics
* invoice, otherwise there is not any program SAPLMR1M!
  CHECK sy-tcode = 'MIRO' OR sy-tcode = 'MIR7'.

* Check assignment via sy-subrc, otherwise
* a short dump occurs when accessing the field symbol
  ASSIGN (c_drseg) TO <ydrseg>.
  IF sy-subrc = 0.
    gt_ydrseg = <ydrseg>.
  ENDIF.

* Local copy gt_ydrseg is only run here,
* the field symbol <ydrseg> should not
* continue to be used!
* The assignment of the current G/L account line in BSEG
* to the line of the original document is carried out via EBELN und
EBELP
  IF NOT bseg-ebeln IS INITIAL AND
     NOT bseg-ebelp IS INITIAL.

    READ TABLE gt_ydrseg INTO gs_ydrseg
        WITH KEY ebeln = bseg-ebeln
                 ebelp = bseg-ebelp.
    IF sy-subrc = 0.
*     ZZ_FELD is a user-defined field in the *    Logistics invoice
      ref_key = gs_ydrseg-zz_feld.
    ENDIF.
  ENDIF.
ENDFORM.
```

Listing 8.6 Transfer of Values from the Original Document

A   User Exits and BAdIs in SAP Materials Management

In this book, you have received numerous examples for using user exits or BAdIs in Materials Management. Nevertheless, it isn't possible to describe all available enhancements in detail. For this reason, this appendix provides a complete list of the user exits, BAdIs, and enhancement spots available in MM.

To structure the large quantity of enhancement options, the appendix is divided into these sections: Purchasing (see Section A.1), External Services Management (see Section A.2), Inventory Management (see Section A.3), Valuation and Account Assignment (see Section A.4), and Logistics Invoice Verification (see Section A.5). Within these sections, the enhancements are summarized as far as possible according to document type or call points and transactions. Otherwise, each section provides the BAdIs first, then the enhancement spots, and finally the enhancements.

Each enhancement is described in the following sections according to the same schema:

► **Type and name**
The following headings may apply:

  ▸ *Enhancement <Name>*
  You can find this enhancement in Transaction SMOD.

  ▸ *BAdI <Name>*
  You can find this BAdI in Transaction SE18.

  ▸ *BAdI <Name> (Enhancement spot <Name>)*
  You can also find this BAdI in Transaction SE18 as an assignment to an enhancement spot.

► **Description of the function**
The function of the enhancement is described in a brief summary. You can see quickly whether this enhancement is suitable for your project. If available, you can find further information in the documentation in the system.

► **Release**
The availability has been checked for each enhancement following Release 4.6C. For enhancements with the note "following SAP R/3 4.6c (or earlier)," it's also possible that these were already available in earlier releases.

▶ **Call points**
Under this entry, you can find transactions, reports, or BAPIs in which this enhancement will run. If an enhancement is able to run from many different transactions, this has been summarized under a general name, for example, "Update Material Documents."

▶ **Methods/components**
The following additional information is provided for each entry:

▶ Especially in the case of BAdIs, the name of the method already bears an initial reference as to which function provides this method. With the quick search for a suitable enhancement, this can be very helpful as an eye-catcher.

▶ The components of an enhancement, for example, EXIT_SAPMM06E_024, are less significant. However, they have been listed to enable a cross-reference from the index to an enhancement.

A.1 Purchasing

Following are all of the enhancement options for the Purchasing area.

A.1.1 Purchase Order Requisitions in General

The following enhancements are provided for the purchase requisitions.

BAdI ME_PROCESS_REQ_CUST

The functionality of Enjoy purchase requisitions can be extensively enhanced via this BAdI. For example, you can run several checks, overwrite the contents of standard fields, or post custom data.

▶ **Release**
From SAP R/3 4.7

▶ **Call points**

▶ Transactions ME51N, ME52N, ME53N, and ME59N

▶ BAPI_PR_CREATE

▶ BAPI_PR_CHANGE

► **Methods**

- ► `INITIALIZE`
- ► `OPEN`
- ► `PROCESS_HEADER`
- ► `PROCESS_ITEM`
- ► `PROCESS_ACCOUNT`
- ► `CHECK`
- ► `POST`
- ► `CLOSE`
- ► `FIELDSELECTION_HEADER_REFKEYS`
- ► `FIELDSELECTION_HEADER`
- ► `FIELDSELECTION_ITEM_REFKEYS`
- ► `FIELDSELECTION_ITEM`

BAdI ME_BAPI_PR_CUST (ES_BADI_ME_BAPI Enhancement Spot)

In this enhancement, you can revise the input and output parameters of the `BAPI_PR_CREATE`, `BAPI_PR_CHANGE`, and `BAPI_PR_GETDETAIL` BAPIs.

► **Release**
from SAP ECC 5.0 (from SAP ECC 6.0 as an enhancement spot)

► **Call points**

- ► `BAPI_PR_CREATE`
- ► `BAPI_PR_CHANGE`
- ► `BAPI_PR_GETDETAIL` (only outbound)

► **Methods**

- ► `INBOUND`
- ► `OUTBOUND`
- ► `MAP2I_EXTENSIONIN`
- ► `MAP2E_EXTENSIONOUT`

BAdI ME_REQ_POSTED

You can use this BAdI to implement any follow-on processing (e.g., the posting of further data or the trigger of a workflow) after updating a purchase requisition.

- **Release**
  from SAP R/3 4.7
- **Call point**
  - Update purchase requisition
- **Method**
  - POSTED

BAdI ME_REQ_HEADER_TEXT

With this BAdI, you can control whether the header text of Enjoy purchase requisitions is copied when purchase requisitions are copied.

- **Release**
  from SAP R/3 4.7
- **Call point**
  - Transaction ME51N
- **Method**
  - COPY_HEADER_TEXT

Enhancement M06B0001

If you set the workflow indicator 9 in a release procedure for a release code, the user exit will run for the role resolution (determination of the responsible person).

- **Release**
  from SAP R/3 4.6C (or earlier)
- **Call point**
  - Purchase requisition release procedure
- **Component**
  - EXIT_SAPLEBNF_001

Enhancement M06B0002

With this enhancement, you can change the content of the `CEBAN` communications structure and therefore influence the release strategy used at the item level.

- ▶ **Release**
  from SAP R/3 4.6C (or earlier)
- ▶ **Call point**
  - ▶ Purchase requisition release procedure
- ▶ **Component**
  - ▶ `EXIT_SAPLEBND_001`

Enhancement M06B0005

With this enhancement, you can change the content of the `CEBAN` communications structure and therefore influence the release strategy used in the overall release.

- ▶ **Release**
  from SAP R/3 4.6C (or earlier)
- ▶ **Call point**
  - ▶ Purchase requisition release procedure
- ▶ **Component**
  - ▶ `EXIT_SAPLEBND_004`

Enhancement M06B0003

In this user exit, you can control the assignment of a custom document number or specify a number range ID that is used when a purchase requisition is generated.

- ▶ **Release**
  from SAP R/3 4.6C (or earlier)
- ▶ **Call points**
  - ▶ Transactions ME51 and ME51N
- ▶ **Component**
  - ▶ `EXIT_SAPMM06B_001`

Enhancement M06B0004

You can use this enhancement to assign a custom document number or to specify a number range ID when a purchase requisition is generated via the `ME_CREATE_REQUISITION_EXT` function module (and, for example, `BAPI_REQUISITION_CREATE` function module).

- **Release**
  from SAP R/3 4.6C (or earlier)
- **Call points**
  - `ME_CREATE_REQUISITION_EXT`
  - `BAPI_REQUISITION_CREATE`
- **Component**
  - `EXIT_SAPLEBNE_001`

Enhancement MEREQ001

This enhancement is used in the purchase requisition to implement custom fields, to update custom tables, or to change standard fields (to a limited extent).

- **Release**
  from SAP R/3 4.6C (or earlier)
- **Call point**
  - Purchase requisition (create, change, display)
- **Components**
  - `EXIT_SAPLMEREQ_001`
  - `EXIT_SAPLMEREQ_002`
  - `EXIT_SAPLMEREQ_003`
  - `EXIT_SAPLMEREQ_004`
  - `EXIT_SAPLMEREQ_005`
  - `EXIT_SAPLMEREQ_006`
  - `EXIT_SAPLMEREQ_007`
  - `EXIT_SAPLMEREQ_008`
  - `EXIT_SAPLMEREQ_009`
  - `EXIT_SAPLMEREQ_010`

- Dynpro 0111 in `SAPLXM02`
- Database include `CI_EBANDB`
- Database include `CI_EBANDBX`
- Database include `CI_EBANMEM`

Enhancement MM06E011

When you implement purchase requisitions via Transaction ME57, these are not locked for performance reasons. If a purchase requisition is changed simultaneously, this can result in an inconsistent purchase requisition commitment. The lock is activated by calling this enhancement. Refer also to SAP Note 378335.

- **Release**
  from SAP R/3 4.6C (or earlier)
- **Call point**
  - Transaction ME57
- **Component**
  - `EXIT_SAPMM06E_024`

A.1.2 Purchase Orders in General

The enhancements listed in this section are provided for purchase orders.

BAdI ME_BAPI_PO_CUST (Enhancement spot ES_BADI_ME_BAPI)

You have the option in this BAdI to revise the input and output parameters of the `BAPI_PO_CREATE1` and `BAPI_PO_CHANGE` BAPIs.

- **Release**
  from SAP ECC 5.0 (from SAP ECC 6.0 as an enhancement spot)
- **Call points**
  - `BAPI_PO_CREATE1`
  - `BAPI_PO_CHANGE`
- **Methods**
  - `INBOUND`
  - `OUTBOUND`
  - `MAP2I_EXTENSIONIN`

- ▶ MAP2E_EXTENSIONOUT
- ▶ TEXT_OUTPUT

BAdI ME_CHECK_ALL_ITEMS

This BAdI can control whether the items are to be rerun when you change the header data in purchase orders, for example, to implement a new pricing.

- ▶ **Release**
  from SAP R/3 4.7
- ▶ **Call points**
  - ▶ Transactions ME21N and ME22N
- ▶ **Method**
  - ▶ RECALCULATE_ITEMS

BAdI ME_HOLD_PO

This BAdI contains an icon via which you can activate or lock the HOLD function in purchase orders. You can find an example of this in Section 2.2, Use of Classic BAdIs, in Chapter 2.

- ▶ **Release**
  from SAP R/3 4.6C (or earlier)
- ▶ **Call points**
  - ▶ Purchase order in Transactions ME21N and ME22N
- ▶ **Method**
  - ▶ IS_ALLOWED

BAdI ME_POHIST_DISP_CUST (ES_BADI_ME_POHIST Enhancement Spot)

With this BAdI, you can customize the purchase order history display in purchase order items according to your custom requirements. You can find an example of this in Section 2.3, Use of New BAdIs (Enhancement Spots), in Chapter 2.

- ▶ **Release**
  from SAP ECC 6.0
- ▶ **Call points**
  - ▶ Purchase orders

▸ **Methods**

- ▸ FIELDCAT_CHANGE
- ▸ OUTTAB_CHANGE
- ▸ HANDLE_HOTSPOT_CLICK

BAdI ME_PURCHDOC_POSTED

You can use this BAdI to implement any follow-on processing (e.g., to post further data or to trigger a workflow) after the purchasing documents have been updated.

▸ **Release**
from SAP R/3 4.7

▸ **Call points**

- ▸ Updating of purchasing documents

▸ **Method**

- ▸ POSTED

BAdI ME_GUI_PO_CUST

This BAdI allows you to define custom dynpros with custom fields in the Enjoy purchase order. Moreover, the implementation of ME_PROCESS_PO_CUST is necessary. You can find an example of this in Section 3.1, Customized Fields in Purchase Orders, in Chapter 3.

▸ **Release**
from SAP R/3 4.7

▸ **Call points**

- ▸ Transactions ME21N, ME22N, and ME23N
- ▸ Transaction ME23N

▸ **Methods**

- ▸ SUBSCRIBE
- ▸ MAP_DYNPRO_FIELDS
- ▸ TRANSPORT_FROM_MODEL
- ▸ TRANSPORT_TO_DYNP
- ▸ TRANSPORT_FROM_DYNP

▶ TRANSPORT_TO_MODEL

▶ EXECUTE

BAdI ME_PROCESS_PO_CUST

With this BAdI, you can extensively enhance the functionality of purchase orders, for example, via custom checks or the processing of custom input fields (see also ME_GUI_PO_CUST BAdI). You can find an example of this in Section 3.1, Customized Fields in Purchase Orders, in Chapter 3.

▶ **Release**
from SAP R/3 4.7

▶ **Call points**

▶ Transactions ME21N, ME22N, and ME23N

▶ Transaction ME29N

▶ BAPI_PO_CREATE1

▶ BAPI_PO_CHANGE

▶ **Methods**

▶ INITIALIZE

▶ OPEN

▶ PROCESS_HEADER

▶ PROCESS_ITEM

▶ PROCESS_SCHEDULE

▶ PROCESS_ACCOUNT

▶ CHECK

▶ POST

▶ CLOSE

▶ FIELDSELECTION_HEADER_REFKEYS

▶ FIELDSELECTION_HEADER

▶ FIELDSELECTION_ITEM_REFKEYS

▶ FIELDSELECTION_ITEM

BAdI ME_TAX_FROM_ADDRESS

You can use this BAdI to determine the tax jurisdiction code with the generation of purchase orders.

▶ **Release**
from SAP R/3 4.7

▶ **Call point**

   ▶ Transaction ME21N

▶ **Methods**

   ▶ GET_TXJCD

   ▶ SERVICES_TXJCD

Enhancement M06E0004

With this user exit, you have the option to change the CEKKO communications structure to influence the release strategy used.

▶ **Release**
from SAP R/3 4.6C (or earlier)

▶ **Call point**

   ▶ Release procedure purchase order

▶ **Component**

   ▶ EXIT_SAPLEBND_002

Enhancement M06E0005

If you set the workflow indicator 9 for a release code in a release procedure, this user exit will run for the role resolution (determination of the person responsible).

▶ **Release**
from SAP R/3 4.6C (or earlier)

▶ **Call point**

   ▶ Release procedure purchase order

▶ **Component**

   ▶ EXIT_SAPLEBNF_005

Enhancement ME590001

With this enhancement, you can define a custom logic for grouping purchase requisitions for purchase order items when purchase requisitions are automatically implemented in purchase orders (ME59).

- ▶ **Release**
  from SAP R/3 4.6C (or earlier)
- ▶ **Call point**
  - ▶ Transaction ME59
- ▶ **Component**
  - ▶ EXIT_SAPLME59_001

Enhancement MM06E004

With this enhancement, the processing of the import data screen can be controlled when the purchasing document is entered.

- ▶ **Release**
  from SAP R/3 4.6C (or earlier)
- ▶ **Call points**
  - ▶ Transactions ME21 and ME21N
- ▶ **Component**
  - ▶ EXIT_SAPMM06E_004

Enhancement MM06E007

With this enhancement, you can control whether a change document is created in the purchase requisition when a purchase requisition is implemented in a purchase order. You can find an example of this in Section 2.1, Use of User Exits, in Chapter 2.

- ▶ **Release**
  from SAP R/3 4.6C (or earlier)
- ▶ **Call points**
  - ▶ Transactions ME21 and ME21N
  - ▶ Transaction ME59

▶ **Component**

    ▶ `EXIT_SAPMM06E_020`

A.1.3   Outline Agreements (Scheduling Agreements/Contracts)

In this section, the following enhancements are provided for scheduling agreements and contracts.

BAdI MEOUT_BAPI_CUST (ES_BADI_ME_BAPI Enhancement Spot)

You can use this BAdI to revise the input and export parameters of the `BAPI_SAG_CREATE`, `BAPI_SAG_CHANGE`, `BAPI_CONTRACT_CREATE`, and `BAPI_CONTRACT_CHANGE` BAPIs.

▶ **Release**
from SAP ECC 6.0

▶ **Call points**

    ▶ `BAPI_SAG_CREATE`

    ▶ `BAPI_SAG_CHANGE`

    ▶ `BAPI_CONTRACT_CREATE`

    ▶ `BAPI_CONTRACT_CHANGE`

▶ **Methods**

    ▶ `INBOUND`

    ▶ `OUTBOUND`

    ▶ `MAP2I_EXTENSIONIN`

    ▶ `MAP2E_EXTENSIONOUT`

BAdI ME_PROCESS_OUT_CUST (ME_PROCESS_OUT Enhancement Spot)

With this BAdI, you can influence the generation of scheduling agreements and contracts if these are generated from the associated BAPIs.

▶ **Release**
from SAP ECC 6.0

▶ **Call points**

    ▶ `BAPI_SAG_CREATE`

    ▶ `BAPI_SAG_CHANGE`

- ▶ BAPI_CONTRACT_CREATE
- ▶ BAPI_CONTRACT_CHANGE

▶ **Methods**

- ▶ INITIALIZE
- ▶ OPEN
- ▶ PROCESS_HEADER
- ▶ PROCESS_ITEM
- ▶ PROCESS_SCHEDULE
- ▶ PROCESS_ACCOUNT
- ▶ CHECK
- ▶ POST
- ▶ CLOSE
- ▶ FIELDSELECTION_HEADER_REFKEYS
- ▶ FIELDSELECTION_HEADER
- ▶ FIELDSELECTION_ITEM_REFKEYS
- ▶ FIELDSELECTION_ITEM

BAdI ME_RELEASE_CREATE

You can use this BAdI to influence the release creation in scheduling agreements. This BAdI replaces the EXIT_SAPLEINL_001 and EXIT_SAPLEINL_002 user exits of the MEETA001 enhancement from earlier releases.

▶ **Release**
from SAP R/3 4.7

▶ **Call points**

- ▶ Scheduling agreements

▶ **Methods**

- ▶ BEFORE_CREATION
- ▶ AFTER_CREATION

BAdI SMOD_MRFLB001

With this BAdI, you can also influence the release creation in scheduling agreements. For example, it allows you to add or delete items, or you can revise the result of the tolerance check.

- **Release**
  from SAP R/3 4.7
- **Call point**
  - Scheduling agreements release creation (Transaction ME84)
- **Methods**
  - EXIT_RM06EFLB_001
  - EXIT_RM06EFLB_002

Enhancement MM06E008

With this enhancement, you can monitor the release value with regard to contract release orders for a value contract and, for example, to display warning or error messages when a specific threshold value has been exceeded.

- **Release**
  from SAP R/3 4.6C (or earlier)
- **Call points**
  - Transactions ME21(N) and ME22(N)
- **Component**
  - EXIT_SAPMM06E_021

Enhancement MMFAB001

This exit runs when scheduling agreement releases are generated (Report RM06EFAB) and provides you with the option to revise the list of selected scheduling agreement items. You can remove and delete items before the releases are finally generated.

- **Release**
  from SAP R/3 4.6C (or earlier)
- **Call point**
  - Report RM06EFAB

- ▶ **Component**
  - ▶ EXIT_RM06EFAB_001

Enhancement MRFLB001

In the RM06EFLB release creation program (Transaction ME84), this user exit is used to revise the scheduling agreement items (see also MMFAB001 enhancement). This enhancement for the SMOD_MRFLB001 BAdI was migrated following Release 4.7.

- ▶ **Release**
  from SAP R/3 4.6C (or earlier)
- ▶ **Call points**
  - ▶ Report RM06EFLB
  - ▶ Transaction ME84
- ▶ **Component**
  - ▶ EXIT_RM06EFLB_001

Enhancement MEETA001

You can use these user exits to influence the release creation in scheduling agreements. This enhancement for the BAdI ME_RELEASE_CREATE was migrated following Release 4.7.

- ▶ **Release**
  following SAP R/3 4.6C (or earlier)
- ▶ **Call points**
  - ▶ Scheduling agreements
- ▶ **Component**
  - ▶ EXIT_SAPLEINL_001

A.1.4 Pricing

The enhancement options listed in this section are used for the pricing in purchasing documents.

BAdI ME_DEFINE_CALCTYPE

With this BAdI, you can specify custom conditions to trigger a new pricing and override the pricing type used.

- **Release**
  from SAP R/3 4.7
- **Call points**
  - Pricing in Transactions ME21N and ME22N
- **Method**
  - DEFINE_CALCTYPE

BAdI ME_PO_PRICING_CUST

You use this BAdI to revise the KOMK and KOMP communications structures, which are the basis of the pricing. In releases earlier than SAP-Basis ECC 6.0, the EXIT_SAPLMEKO_001 (enhancement LMEKO001) and EXIT_SAPLMEKO_002 (enhancement LMEKO002) user exits are alternatively provided.

- **Release**
  from SAP ECC 6.0
- **Call points**
  - Pricing in Transactions ME21N and ME22N
- **Methods**
  - PROCESS_KOMK
  - PROCESS_KOMP

Enhancement LMEKO001

You can use this enhancement to revise the KOMK communications structure, which is a basis of the pricing. Following SAP ECC 6.0, the ME_PO_PRICING_CUST BAdI is alternatively provided.

- **Release**
  from SAP R/3 4.6C (or earlier)
- **Call points**
  - Pricing in Transactions ME21(N) and ME22(N)
- **Component**
  - EXIT_SAPLMEKO_001

Enhancement LMEKO002

You can use this enhancement to revise the KOMP communications structure, which is the basis of the pricing. Following SAP ECC 6.0, the ME_PO_PRICING_CUST BAdI is alternatively provided.

- **Release**
  from SAP R/3 4.6C (or earlier)

- **Call points**
  - Pricing in Transactions ME21(N) and ME22(N)

- **Component**
  - EXIT_SAPLMEKO_002

Enhancement LMEXF001

With this user exit, you can control whether conditions on an item can be maintained in purchase order and outline agreements, even when no invoice receipt is allowed.

- **Release**
  from SAP R/3 4.6C (or earlier)

- **Call points**
  - Transactions ME21(N) and ME22(N)
  - Transactions ME31K and ME32K
  - Transactions ME31L and ME32L

- **Component**
  - EXIT_SAPLMEXF_001

A.1.5   Commitment Functions

The enhancements in this section are provided for commitment management in MM.

BAdI ME_COMMITMENT_PLAN
(ES_COMMITMENT_PLAN Enhancement Spot)

With this BAdI, you can change a commitment plan for contracts or store custom checks. When you create a commitment plan, you can set it up completely with default values.

- **Release**
from SAP ECC 6.0
- **Call point**
  - Contract
- **Methods**
  - OPEN
  - PROCESS

BAdI ME_COMMITMENT_RETURN

With this BAdI, you can use the commitment functions for return items in purchase orders to return the value of the item again to the budget.

- **Release**
following SAP ECC 6.0
- **Call points**
  - Purchase orders
- **Method**
  - IS_ACTIVE

BAdI ME_REQ_OI_EXT

With this BAdI, you can specify whether a commitment update follows when purchase requisitions are created and changed from foreign applications.

- **Release**
from SAP R/3 4.7
- **Call points**
  - Purchase requisitions
- **Method**
  - IS_REQUESTED

A.1.6   Cross-Document

The following enhancements are used from various purchasing documents and cannot be assigned to one of the previous groups.

BAdI ME_CHDOC_ACTIVE

This BAdI is used to additionally update changes to document conditions, document links, subcontractor components, or export/import data.

▶ **Release**
from SAP R/3 4.7

▶ **Call points**

  ▶ Purchasing documents (query, quotation, purchase order, contract, scheduling agreement)

  ▶ Purchase requisitions (only document links and subcontractor components)

▶ **Method**

  ▶ IS_ACTIVE

BAdI ME_CIP_ALLOW_CHANGE

You can use this BAdI to control the changeability of configuration data in purchasing documents and purchase requisitions.

▶ **Release**
from SAP R/3 4.7

▶ **Call points**

  ▶ Purchasing documents configuration

  ▶ Purchase requisitions configuration

▶ **Method**

  ▶ GET_DISPLAY

MEQUERY1 Enhancement

With this enhancement, you can enhance the document overview in purchase requisitions using custom selection variants, enhance or remove standard selections, or store custom display variants. You can find an example of this in Section 3.2, Customization of the Document Overview in Purchase Requisitions or Purchase Orders, in Chapter 2.

▶ **Release**
from SAP R/3 4.6C (or earlier)

- ▶ **Call points**
  - ▶ Purchase requisitions
  - ▶ Purchase orders
- ▶ **Components**
  - ▶ EXIT_SAPLMEQUERY_001
  - ▶ EXIT_SAPLMEQUERY_002

LMEQR001 Enhancement

This user exit runs in the source. The number of possible sources found can then be reduced to just one.

- ▶ **Release**
  from SAP R/3 4.6C (or earlier)
- ▶ **Call point**
  - ▶ Source
- ▶ **Component**
  - ▶ EXIT_SAPLMEQR_001

LWSUS001 Enhancement

This enhancement provides the option to implement a custom source.

- ▶ **Release**
  from SAP R/3 4.6C (or earlier)
- ▶ **Call point**
  - ▶ Source
- ▶ **Component**
  - ▶ EXIT_SAPLWSUS_001

MM06E003 Enhancement

This enhancement is used to assign a custom document number or to specify a number range ID when a purchasing document is generated.

- ▶ **Release**
  from SAP R/3 4.6C (or earlier)

- ▶ **Call points**
  - ▶ Purchasing documents
- ▶ **Component**
  - ▶ EXIT_SAPMM06E_001

Enhancement MM06E005

You can define custom fields in the purchasing documents at header and item level using this enhancement. The data is usually attached as an include structure to Table EKKO (CI_EKKODB structure) or Table EKPO (CI_EKPODB structure). If required, you can also update data in custom tables.

- ▶ **Release**
  from SAP R/3 4.6C (or earlier)
- ▶ **Call points**
  - ▶ Purchasing documents
- ▶ **Components**
  - ▶ EXIT_SAPMM06E_006
  - ▶ EXIT_SAPMM06E_007
  - ▶ EXIT_SAPMM06E_008
  - ▶ EXIT_SAPMM06E_009
  - ▶ EXIT_SAPMM06E_012
  - ▶ EXIT_SAPMM06E_013
  - ▶ EXIT_SAPMM06E_014
  - ▶ EXIT_SAPMM06E_016
  - ▶ EXIT_SAPMM06E_017
  - ▶ EXIT_SAPMM06E_018

MM06E009 Enhancement

An icon appears in the purchasing documents at item level as soon as item texts are available. With this enhancement, you can control for which type of texts this icon appears.

- ▶ **Release**
  from SAP R/3 4.6C (or earlier)

- **Call points**
  - Purchasing documents
- **Component**
  - EXIT_SAPMM06E_022

MM06E010 Enhancement

The field control of fields of the vendor address in purchasing document is only possible to a slight extent in Customizing. This user exit provides you with complete flexibility to control these fields if required.

- **Release**
  from SAP R/3 4.6C (or earlier)
- **Call points**
  - Purchasing documents
- **Component**
  - EXIT_SAPMM06E_005

MMDA0001 Enhancement

The MMDA0001 enhancement is used for the custom proposal of the delivery address in purchasing documents. In the standard system, the delivery address is determined via the combination plant/storage — if no storage location address is maintained, the plant address is suggested.

- **Release**
  from SAP R/3 4.6C (or earlier)
- **Call points**
  - Purchasing documents
- **Component**
  - EXIT_SAPLMMDA_001

A.1.7 Vendor Evaluation

Enhancement options for vendor evaluations are presented in this section.

MM06L001 Enhancement

It's possible via the user exits of this enhancement to overwrite the scores determined in the standard for both the general and quality criteria of the vendor evaluation through the results of custom logic.

- ▶ **Release**
  from SAP R/3 4.6C (or earlier)

- ▶ **Call points**
  - ▶ Transaction ME61
  - ▶ Transaction ME63
  - ▶ Transaction ME65

- ▶ **Components**
  - ▶ `EXIT_RM06LBAT_001`
  - ▶ `EXIT_RM06LBEW_001`
  - ▶ `EXIT_SAPLMEL0_001`
  - ▶ `EXIT_SAPMM06L_001`

A.1.8   IDoc Processing

The enhancements for IDocs are provided in EDI processing.

BAdI MM_EDI_DESADV_IN

In the EDI inbound processing, you can enhance inbound deliveries with `DESADV` type (`DELVRY01` basic IDoc).

- ▶ **Release**
  from SAP R/3 4.7

- ▶ **Call point**
  - ▶ `IDOC_INPUT_DESADV1`

- ▶ **Method**
  - ▶ `PROCESS_KOMDLGN_PO`

LMELA010 Enhancement

With this enhancement, you can copy additional fields from the IDoc with the inbound processing of an IDoc to generate a shipping notification that is not usually copied (e.g., the batch).

- ▶ **Release**
  from SAP R/3 4.6C (or earlier)
- ▶ **Call point**
  - ▶ `IDOC_INPUT_DESADV1`
- ▶ **Component**
  - ▶ `EXIT_SAPLEINM_010`

MM06E001 Enhancement

With this enhancement, you can influence the inbound and outbound data of IDocs or enhance segments. In the inbound processing, you have access to the `ORDRSP` (order confirmation) and `DESADV` (shipping notification) messages. In the outbound processing, the messages are `ORDERS` (outgoing purchase order), `ORDCHG` (purchase order change notice), `REQOTE` (query), and `DELFOR` and `DELINS` (scheduling agreement schedule). Moreover, `BLAREL` (release documentation) is provided in the inbound and outbound processing.

- ▶ **Release**
  from SAP R/3 4.6C (or earlier)
- ▶ **Call point**
  - ▶ IDoc inbound processing/outbound processing (see description)
- ▶ **Components**
  - ▶ `EXIT_SAPLEINM_001`
  - ▶ `EXIT_SAPLEINM_002`
  - ▶ `EXIT_SAPLEINM_003`
  - ▶ `EXIT_SAPLEINM_004`
  - ▶ `EXIT_SAPLEINM_005`
  - ▶ `EXIT_SAPLEINM_006`
  - ▶ `EXIT_SAPLEINM_007`
  - ▶ `EXIT_SAPLEINM_008`
  - ▶ `EXIT_SAPLEINM_009`

A.1.9 Logistics Information Systems

In the Logistics Information System (LIS), the following enhancements are provided.

LWBON001 Enhancement

You can use this enhancement to enrich the LIS update by enhancing the MCKONA communications structure (sales and revenues).

- **Release**
  from SAP R/3 4.6C (or earlier)

- **Call point**

  - LIS updating

- **Components**

  - EXIT_SAPLWN08_001

  - EXIT_SAPLWN12_001

  - EXIT_SAPLWN35_001

A.1.10 Archiving

The enhancement options presented in this section are for archiving purchasing documents.

BAdI ARC_MM_EBAN_PRECHECK

In this BAdI, you can execute custom checks in the preprocessing program on the archivability of purchase requisitions.

- **Release**
  following SAP ECC 6.0

- **Call point**

  - Preprocessing Program RM06BV70

- **Method**

  - CHECK

BAdI ARC_MM_EBAN_CHECK

In this BAdI, you can execute custom checks on the archivability of purchase requisitions in the write program.

- **Release**
  from SAP ECC 6.0
- **Call point**
  - Write Program RM06BW70
- **Method**
  - CHECK

BAdI ARC_MM_EBAN_WRITE

With this BAdI, you can enhance the volume of archiving of the write and deletion program for purchase requisitions with other database tables (e.g., also archiving with custom tables with custom data).

- **Release**
  from SAP ECC 6.0
- **Call points**
  - Write Program RM06BW70
  - Deletion Program RM06BD70
- **Methods**
  - WRITE
  - DELETE

BAdI ARC_MM_EINA_CHECK

This BAdI is provided for custom checks for the archivability in the write program of purchasing information records.

- **Release**
  from SAP ECC 6.0
- **Call point**
  - Write Program RM06IW47
- **Method**
  - CHECK

BAdI ARC_MM_EINA_WRITE

With this BAdI, you can enhance the volume of archiving of the write and deletion program for purchasing information records with other database tables (e.g., custom tables with custom data).

- **Release**
  from SAP ECC 6.0
- **Call points**
  - Write Program RM06IW47
  - Deletion Program RM06ID47
- **Methods**
  - WRITE
  - DELETE

BAdI ARC_MM_EKKO_CHECK

This BAdI is used to execute custom checks for the archivability in the write program of purchase orders.

- **Release**
  from SAP ECC 6.0
- **Call point**
  - Write Program RM06EW47
- **Method**
  - CHECK

BAdI ARC_MM_EKKO_WRITE

With this BAdI, you can enhance the volume of archiving of the write and deletion program for purchase orders with other database tables (e.g., custom tables with custom data). Further information is contained in SAP Note 673030.

- **Release**
  from SAP ECC 6.0
- **Call points**
  - Write Program RM06EW47
  - Deletion Program RM06ED47

▶ **Methods**

   ▸ WRITE

   ▸ DELETE

A.2 External Services Management

In External Services Management, you have the enhancement options shown in this section.

BAdI MMSRV_SM_BAPI_CUST

In this BAdI, two methods are provided to change the data of the BAPI interface in the inbound and outbound processing if required.

▶ **Release**
from SAP ECC 6.0

▶ **Call points**

   ▸ BAPI_SERVICE_CREATE

   ▸ BAPI_SERVICE_CHANGE

▶ **Methods**

   ▸ INBOUND

   ▸ OUTBOUND

BAdI MMSRV_SM_MAIN

The methods of this BAdI run while the service master data is processed when the call follows via the previously mentioned BAPIs.

▶ **Release**
from SAP ECC 6.0

▶ **Call points**

   ▸ BAPI_SERVICE_CREATE

   ▸ BAPI_SERVICE_CHANGE

▶ **Methods**

   ▸ PROCESS_SSC_DATA

   ▸ PROCESS_CUST_DATA

BAdI MMSRV_SM_NOTIFY

The NOTIFY method always runs when a service master data record is created or changed. The method can be used to send a message if a change has taken place in the service master.

▸ **Release**
from SAP ECC 6.0

▸ **Call points**

  ▸ Transaction AC03

  ▸ BAPI_SERVICE_CREATE

  ▸ BAPI_SERVICE_CHANGE

  ▸ IDOC_INPUT_SRVMAS

▸ **Method**

  ▸ NOTIFY

BASO0001 Enhancement

With the exit of this enhancement, you can revise the IDoc data when sending service master data.

▸ **Release**
from SAP R/3 4.6C (or earlier)

▸ **Call point**

  ▸ IDoc outbound processing service master

▸ **Components**

  ▸ EXIT_SAPLBASO_001

  ▸ EXIT_SAPLBASO_002

Enhancement SRVDET

This enhancement is used to integrate custom fields into the service entry detail screen. The data can be attached via the CI_ESLLDB append to the ESLL table.

▸ **Release**
from SAP R/3 4.6C (or earlier)

▸ **Call point**

  ▸ Transaction ML81N

▶ **Components**

  ▶ EXIT_SAPLMLSP_040

  ▶ EXIT_SAPLMLSP_041

SRVEDIT Enhancement

Using this exit controls whether the user can change the service specification in the service entry sheet.

▶ **Release**
  from SAP R/3 4.6C (or earlier)

▶ **Call point**

  ▶ Transaction ML81N

▶ **Component**

  ▶ EXIT_SAPLMLSR_001

SRVESI Enhancement

For the import or export of service data from or to external systems, the interface data in these user exits is provided for processing.

▶ **Release**
  from SAP R/3 4.6C (or earlier)

▶ **Call points**

  ▶ Transaction ML86

  ▶ Transaction ML87

▶ **Components**

  ▶ EXIT_SAPLMLSX_002

  ▶ EXIT_SAPLMLSX_003

SRVESKN Enhancement

With this enhancement, an account assignment can be specified for new service lines. For multiple account assignments, the percentage or quantity amount can also be provided. You can find an example of this in Section 4.1, Prepopulating Account Assignment for Service Lines, in Chapter 4.

▶ **Release**
  from SAP R/3 4.6C (or earlier)

- ▶ **Call points**
  - ▶ Relevant purchasing documents
- ▶ **Component**
  - ▶ EXIT_SAPLMLSK_001

SRVESLL Enhancement

It is possible to check the input of the service lines via the user exits of this enhancement (ESLL structure/table). You can find an example of this in Section 4.2, Input Check of the Service Lines, in Chapter 4.

- ▶ **Release**
  from SAP R/3 4.6C (or earlier)
- ▶ **Call points**
  - ▶ Relevant purchasing documents
- ▶ **Components**
  - ▶ EXIT_SAPLMLSP_030
  - ▶ EXIT_SAPLMLSP_031

SRVESSR Enhancement

When you create an entry sheet, you can prepopulate the header data using this enhancement (ESSR structure/table). You can find an example of this in Section 4.3, Prepopulation of the Header Data in the Data Entry Sheet, in Chapter 4.

- ▶ **Release**
  from SAP R/3 4.6C (or earlier)
- ▶ **Call point**
  - ▶ Transaction ML81N
- ▶ **Component**
  - ▶ EXIT_SAPLMLSR_010

SRVEUSCR Enhancement

This enhancement enables the integration of custom fields at the header data level of the entry sheet. Data can be saved via an (CI_ESSRDB) append for the ESSR table.

- ▸ **Release**
  from SAP R/3 4.6C (or earlier)
- ▸ **Call point**
  - ▸ Transaction ML81N
- ▸ **Components**
  - ▸ EXIT_SAPLMLSR_020
  - ▸ EXIT_SAPLMLSR_021
  - ▸ Dynpro SAPLXMLU 0399

SRVKNTTP Enhancement

With an external creation of an entry sheet, an account assignment type U (unknown) may possibly exist, which can result in problems. The account assignment type can be specified using this enhancement.

- ▸ **Release**
  from SAP R/3 4.6C (or earlier)
- ▸ **Call point**
  - ▸ Transaction ML87
- ▸ **Component**
  - ▸ EXIT_SAPLMLSX_001

SRVLIMIT Enhancement

You have the option to execute a custom limit check. Display an error message in the user exit to reject the input of the user.

- ▸ **Release**
  from SAP R/3 4.6C (or earlier)
- ▸ **Call point**
  - ▸ Transaction ML81N
- ▸ **Component**
  - ▸ EXIT_SAPLMLSL_001

SRVMAIL1 Enhancement

Although this enhancement is still available, it should no longer be used. The SRVESI enhancement has existed since Release 4.0B, which provides a wider scope of functions.

- ▶ **Release**
  from SAP R/3 4.6C (or earlier)

- ▶ **Call points**
  - ▶ Transaction ML86
  - ▶ Transaction ML87

- ▶ **Components**
  - ▶ EXIT_SAPLMLSX_010
  - ▶ EXIT_SAPLMLSX_011

SRVMSTLV Enhancement

Using the user exit of this enhancement, you can convert the units of measure when a standard service catalog is read from a file.

- ▶ **Release**
  from SAP R/3 4.6C (or earlier)

- ▶ **Call point**
  - ▶ Transaction MLS5

- ▶ **Component**
  - ▶ EXIT_SAPLMLST_001

SRVREL Enhancement

Using this enhancement, you can change the CESSR communications structure to influence the release strategy used for an entry sheet.

- ▶ **Release**
  from SAP R/3 4.6C (or earlier)

- ▶ **Call point**
  - ▶ Transaction ML81N

- ▶ **Component**
  - ▶ EXIT_SAPLEBND_003

SRVSEL Enhancement

If you trigger the `SELECTION_POSSIBLE` exception via `RAISE` in `EXIT_SAPLMLSP_010`, the COPY FROM NON-SAP SYSTEM function appears in the menu on the service selection. After you have selected this function, the `EXIT_SAPLMLSP_011` function modules are executed, and service data can be copied to the directory.

- ▶ **Release**
  from SAP R/3 4.6C (or earlier)
- ▶ **Call points**
  - ▶ Transactions ME21N/ME22N
  - ▶ Transaction ML81N
- ▶ **Components**
  - ▶ `EXIT_SAPLMLSP_010`
  - ▶ `EXIT_SAPLMLSP_011`

A.3 Inventory Management

The following enhancement options are available in the area of Inventory Management.

A.3.1 Material Documents in General

The following enhancements are provided for material documents in this section.

BAdI MB_DOCUMENT_BADI

In the `MB_DOCUMENT_BEFORE_UPDATE` method, you can call custom update modules to post additional data. You should avoid, where possible, using the `MB_DOCUMENT_UPDATE` method, which already runs automatically in the update and therefore allows the direct update in database tables for performance reasons.

- ▶ **Release**
  from SAP R/3 4.6C (or earlier)
- ▶ **Call point**
  - ▶ Material document update

- ▶ **Methods**
  - ▶ MB_DOCUMENT_BEFORE_UPDATE
  - ▶ MB_DOCUMENT_UPDATE

BAdI MB_MIGO_ITEM_BADI

In Transaction MIGO, you can use this BAdI to automatically fill the item text (SGTXT field) or to suggest the storage location. It is also possible to execute input checks in standard fields. For this, all data of the material document is provided. You can find an example of this in Section 5.3, Checking and Prepopulating Standard Fields, in Chapter 5.

- ▶ **Release**
  from SAP R/3 4.7
- ▶ **Call point**
  - ▶ Transaction MIGO, item entry
- ▶ **Method**
  - ▶ ITEM_MODIFY

BAdI MB_MIGO_BADI

MB_MIGO_BADI is a very comprehensive BAdI for implementing tabstrips with custom data at the header and item level. It's also possible to execute custom input checks in standard fields and prepopulate some standard fields. You can find an example of this in Sections 5.1, Custom Fields in Transaction MIGO, and 5.2, Other Functions of the BAdI MB_MIGO_BADI, in Chapter 5.

- ▶ **Release**
  from SAP R/3 4.7
- ▶ **Call point**
  - ▶ Transaction MIGO
- ▶ **Methods**
  - ▶ INIT
  - ▶ PBO_DETAIL
  - ▶ PAI_DETAIL
  - ▶ LINE_MODIFY
  - ▶ LINE_DELETE

- ▶ RESET

- ▶ POST_DOCUMENT

- ▶ CHECK_ITEM

- ▶ MODE_SET

- ▶ STATUS_AND_HEADER

- ▶ HOLD_DATA_SAVE

- ▶ HOLD_DATA_LOAD

- ▶ HOLD_DATA_DELETE

- ▶ PBO_HEADER

- ▶ PAI_HEADER

- ▶ CHECK_HEADER

- ▶ PUBLISH_MATERIAL_ITEM

BAdI MB_CHECK_LINE_BADI

This BAdI runs for each item directly prior to inclusion in the lock table and can be used to execute custom checks.

- ▶ **Release**
  from SAP R/3 4.7

- ▶ **Call point**
  - ▶ Material document item entry

- ▶ **Method**
  - ▶ CHECK_LINE

BAdI MB_INSMK_WIP_CHANGE (MB_GOODSMOVEMENT Enhancement Spot)

When reposting a WIP batch (Work in Progress; see documentation on the LOG_PP_WIP_BATCH business function), you can change the stock type using this BAdI and therefore repost the batch to the blocked stock.

- ▶ **Release**
  from SAP ECC 6.0 (Enhancement Package 4, LOG_MM_OM_1 Business Function)

- ▶ **Call point**
  - ▶ Transaction MIGO

- **Method**
  - CHANGE_WIP_INSMK_TO_BLOCKED

MB_CF001 Enhancement

This module is called in the update of the material document directly prior to COMMIT WORK and is used to call custom update modules (to update custom tables). Alternatively, you can also the MB_DOCUMENT_BADI enhancement for this.

- **Release**
  from SAP R/3 4.6C (or earlier)
- **Call point**
  - Material document update
- **Component**
  - EXIT_SAPLMBMB_001

MBCF0002 Enhancement

In this enhancement, various pieces of information from the header and item level of the document are provided to fill the item text (SGTXT field) when document items are entered. The item text is copied to the field of the accounting document of the same name. From Release 4.7, you can use instead the MB_MIGO_ITEM_BADI enhancement (only Transaction MIGO).

- **Release**
  from SAP R/3 4.6C (or earlier)
- **Call point**
  - Material document item entry
- **Component**
  - EXIT_SAPMM07M_001

MBCF0005 Enhancement

Using this enhancement, you can overwrite standard text elements for printing goods receipt/issue slip or to fill custom fields of the transfer structure to display these on a goods receipt/issue slip.

- **Release**
  from SAP R/3 4.6C (or earlier)

▶ **Call point**

▶ Material document item entry

▶ **Components**

▶ `EXIT_SAPM07DR_001`

▶ `EXIT_SAPM07DR_002`

MBCF0009 Enhancement

If a storage location is necessary to enter document items from a dialog transaction, this enhancement will run, and you can specify the storage location according to a custom logic. From Release 4.7, you can use instead the `MB_MIGO_ITEM_BADI` enhancement (only Transaction MIGO).

▶ **Release**
from SAP R/3 4.6C (or earlier)

▶ **Call point**

▶ Material document item entry

▶ **Component**

▶ `EXIT_SAPMM07M_009`

MBCFC003 Enhancement

If a new batch is specified for a material movement, this enhancement will run. You have the option to overwrite some information on the batch master and to use it for the creation.

▶ **Release**
from SAP R/3 4.6C (or earlier)

▶ **Call point**

▶ Material document batch entry

▶ **Component**

▶ `EXIT_SAPMM07M_003`

MBCFC004 Enhancement

If a material movement is executed with a batch reference, you can evaluate the free characteristics of the batch in this enhancement.

- ▶ **Release**
  from SAP R/3 4.6C (or earlier)

- ▶ **Call point**

  - ▶ Material document batch entry

- ▶ **Component**

  - ▶ EXIT_SAPMM07M_004

IQSM0007 Enhancement

If you work with serial numbers, this user exit can be used to prepare data of the material document in the function group of the exit so that the latter can be used in other user exits. A sensible usage is therefore only possible when combined with other enhancements of the serial number management. Further details can be found in the documentation of this enhancement.

- ▶ **Release**
  from SAP R/3 4.6C (or earlier)

- ▶ **Call point**

  - ▶ Material document update

- ▶ **Component**

  - ▶ EXIT_SAPLIE01_007

XMBF0001 Enhancement

These two user exits always run when a stock determination is performed. You have the option to set the stock determination rule and to customize the stock determination item table if required.

- ▶ **Release**
  from SAP R/3 4.6C (or earlier)

- ▶ **Call point**

  - ▶ Stock determination

- ▶ **Components**

  - ▶ EXIT_SAPLMDBF_001

  - ▶ EXIT_SAPLMDBF_002

A.3.2   Goods Receipt

To post goods receipts, you have the enhancement options presented in this section.

BAdI MB_GOODSMOVEMENT_DCI
(MB_GOODSMOVEMENT Enhancement Spot)

With this BAdI, you have the option via custom logic to determine whether and when the inward delivery completed indicator of a purchase order is to be set.

▶ **Release**
from SAP ECC 6.0 (Enhancement Package 4, Business Function `LOG_MMFI_P2P`)

▶ **Call points**

  ▶ Transaction MIGO

  ▶ Transaction MB01

▶ **Method**

  ▶ `SET_DCI`

BAdI MB_ACCOUNTING_DISTRIBUTE
(MB_GOODSMOVEMENT Enhancement Spot)

During the processing of goods receipt items with multiple account assignments, you can specify the distribution to the individual account assignment objects using this BAdI.

▶ **Release**
from SAP ECC 6.0 (Enhancement Package 4, Business Function `LOG_MM_MAA_1`)

▶ **Call points**

  ▶ Transaction MIGO

  ▶ Transaction MB01

▶ **Method**

  ▶ `CHANGE_DISTRIBUTION`

LMELA002 Enhancement

This enhancement is used to copy a batch number from the shipping notification to the goods receipt. For this, the `LMELA010` enhancement is necessary, through which you copy the batch number to a shipping notification (enhancement in purchasing; see Section A.1.8, IDoc Processing).

- **Release**
  from SAP R/3 4.6C (or earlier)

- **Call points**
  - Transaction MIGO
  - Transaction MB01

- **Component**
  - EXIT_SAPLEINR_002

MBCF0006 Enhancement

When you post a goods receipt for a subcontractor purchase order, this enhancement runs during the determination of the subcontracting components to be cleared. You have the option here to influence the WBS element (element of the project structure) to be posted for this operation.

- **Release**
  from SAP R/3 4.6C (or earlier)

- **Call points**
  - Transaction MIGO
  - Transaction MB01

- **Components**
  - EXIT_SAPLMIGO_001
  - EXIT_SAPMM07M_005

MEFLD004 Enhancement

This user exit is run when posting a goods receipt for a purchase order. You can specify the earliest delivery date, and therefore reject a goods receipt if required. You can find an example of this in Section 5.4, Check of the Earliest Delivery Date, in Chapter 5.

- **Release**
  from SAP R/3 4.6C (or earlier)

- ▶ **Call points**
  - ▶ Transaction MIGO
  - ▶ Transaction MB01
- ▶ **Component**
  - ▶ EXIT_SAPLEINR_004

MEVME001 Enhancement

These user exits run when posting a goods receipt for a scheduling agreement. Using the scheduling agreement, you can specify the default quantity for the goods receipt to be posted and overwrite the quantity that the tolerance check will refer to. You can find an example of this in Section 5.5, Tolerance Limits for Scheduling Agreements, in Chapter 5.

- ▶ **Release**
  from SAP R/3 4.6C (or earlier)
- ▶ **Call points**
  - ▶ Transaction MIGO
  - ▶ Transaction MB01
- ▶ **Components**
  - ▶ EXIT_SAPLEINR_001
  - ▶ EXIT_SAPLEINR_003

A.3.3   Reservations

The following enhancement options are provided for reservations.

BAdI MB_RESERVATION_BADI

Using this BAdI, you have the option to prepopulate fields with values or to check the data entered by the user, and to display error messages if applicable. You can find an example of this in Section 5.6, Enhancement of Reservations, in Chapter 5.

- ▶ **Release**
  from SAP R/3 4.7
- ▶ **Call points**
  - ▶ Transactions MB21 and MB22

- ▶ **Methods**
  - ▶ DATA_MODIFY
  - ▶ DATA_CHECK

MBCF0007 Enhancement

This enhancement is run during the update of reservations and can also be used to update custom tables. Changes to standard tables should no longer be implemented at this point.

- ▶ **Release**
  from SAP R/3 4.6C (or earlier)
- ▶ **Call points**
  - ▶ Transactions MB21 and MB22
- ▶ **Component**
  - ▶ EXIT_SAPMM07R_001

A.3.4 Archiving

The following enhancement options are for archiving inventory and material documents.

BAdI ARC_MM_MATBEL_CHECK

The CHECK method of this BAdI runs in the write program for the MM_MATBEL archiving object (material documents). Using custom criteria, you have the option here to check whether the archivability for a document has been specified.

- ▶ **Release**
  from SAP R/3 4.7
- ▶ **Call point**
  - ▶ Write Program RM07MARCS
- ▶ **Method**
  - ▶ CHECK

BAdI ARC_MM_MATBEL_WRITE

The methods of this BAdI run in the write and deletion program for the MM_MATBEL archiving object (material documents) and are used to process additional (custom) data.

- ► **Release**
  from SAP R/3 4.7

- ► **Call points**
  - ► Write Program RM07MARCS
  - ► Deletion Program RM07MADES

- ► **Methods**
  - ► PREPARE_WRITE
  - ► WRITE
  - ► DELETE

BAdI ARC_MM_INVBEL_CHECK

The CHECK method of this BAdI runs in the write program for the MM_INVBEL archiving object (inventory documents). Using custom criteria, you can check whether the archivability for a document has been specified.

- ► **Release**
  from SAP ECC 6.0

- ► **Call point**
  - ► Write Program RM07IARCS

- ► **Method**
  - ► CHECK

BAdI ARC_MM_INVBEL_WRITE

The methods of this BAdI run in the write and deletion programs for the MM_INVBEL archiving object (inventory documents) and are used to process additional (custom) data.

- ► **Release**
  from SAP ECC 6.0

- ▶ **Call points**
  - ▶ Write Program RM07IARCS
  - ▶ Deletion Program RM07IDELS
- ▶ **Methods**
  - ▶ WRITE
  - ▶ DELETE

A.4 Valuation and Account Assignment

The following enhancement options exist in the area of valuation and account assignment.

LIFO0040 Enhancement

With this enhancement, the LIFO valuation (last-in/first-out) can be influenced. Among these is the assignment of material numbers for material pools, the influencing of the pool-splitting procedure, and the lowest value comparison.

- ▶ **Release**
  from SAP R/3 4.6C (or earlier)
- ▶ **Call points**
  - ▶ Transactions MRF1 and MRF3
- ▶ **Components**
  - ▶ EXIT_SAPLLIFS_001
  - ▶ EXIT_SAPLLIFS_002
  - ▶ EXIT_SAPLLIFS_003

NIWE0000 Enhancement

In the balance sheet valuation, you can change or replace stock quantities, consumption quantities, and goods received quantities using this enhancement.

- ▶ **Release**
  from SAP R/3 4.6C (or earlier)
- ▶ **Call point**
  - ▶ Transaction MRF1

▸ **Components**

- ▸ EXIT_SAPLNIWE_003
- ▸ EXIT_SAPLNIWE_004
- ▸ EXIT_SAPLNIWE_005

NIWE0001 Enhancement

By influencing the market price analysis with regard to determination of lowest value, you can exclude purchasing documents, override document types, or completely change the determined market price.

▸ **Release**
from SAP R/3 4.6C (or earlier)

▸ **Call point**

- ▸ Transaction MRF1

▸ **Components**

- ▸ EXIT_SAPLNIW0_001
- ▸ EXIT_SAPLNIW0_002
- ▸ EXIT_SAPLNIW0_003

NIWE0002 Enhancement

In this enhancement, you can influence the procedures for coverage and movement rate with regard to the lowest value determination. This includes changing the devaluation percentages, the devaluation indicators, or the creation date of the material masters, excluding the materials of the devaluation.

▸ **Release**
from SAP R/3 4.6C (or earlier)

▸ **Call point**

- ▸ Transaction MRF1

▸ **Components**

- ▸ EXIT_SAPLNIW1_001
- ▸ EXIT_SAPLNIW1_002
- ▸ EXIT_SAPLNIWE_001

Enhancement NIWE0003

This enhancement is used to influence the loss-free valuation in the lowest value determination. For this, essential account determination keys can be changed.

▶ **Release**
from SAP R/3 4.6C (or earlier)

▶ **Call point**
  ▶ Transaction MRF1

▶ **Components**
  ▶ EXIT_SAPLNIW3_001
  ▶ EXIT_SAPLNIW3_002

LMR1M002 Enhancement

With this enhancement, an override of the account modification constant for the GR/IR account determination and of the GR/IR account is possible. You can find an example of this in Section 6.1, GR/IR Account, in Chapter 6.

▶ **Release**
from SAP R/3 4.6C (or earlier)

▶ **Call points**
  ▶ Goods receipt posting
  ▶ Invoice verification (Transactions MIRO and MR1M)

▶ **Component**
  ▶ EXIT_SAPLKONT_011

A.5 Logistics Invoice Verification

The following enhancements are provided in Logistics Invoice Verification.

A.5.1 General

You have the following enhancement options when you generate logistics incoming invoices.

BAdI MRM_ERS_HDAT_MODIFY

With the automatic invoicing of delivery costs in the ERS procedure (Evaluated Receipt Settlement), this BAdI is provided to partly revise the header data of the document to be generated.

► **Release**
from SAP ECC 6.0

► **Call point**

  ► Report RMMR1MDC

► **Method**

  ► ERS_HEADERDATA_MODIFY

BAdI MRM_ERS_IDAT_MODIFY

With the automatic invoicing of planned delivery costs in the ERS procedure (Evaluated Receipt Settlement), this BAdI is provided to revise the document lines of the document to be processed.

► **Release**
from SAP ECC 6.0

► **Call points**

  ► Report RMMR1MDC (Transaction MRDC)

  ► Report RMMR1MRS (Transaction MRRL)

► **Method**

  ► ERS_ITEMDATA_MODIFY

BAdI MRM_ITEM_CUSTFIELDS

This BAdI allows you to implement a custom tab so that you can manage custom fields at item level. You can find an example of this in Section 7.1, Custom Fields in Transaction MIRO, in Chapter 7.

► **Release**
from SAP ECC 6.0

► **Call points**

  ► Transaction MIRO

  ► Transaction MIR7

- ▶ **Methods**
  - ▶ TABPAGE_LABEL_SET
  - ▶ CUSTOMDATA_MODIFY
  - ▶ INVOICE_DATA_TRANSFER
  - ▶ CUSTOM_DATA_TRANSFER
  - ▶ CUSTOM_DATA_GET
  - ▶ INVOICE_DATA_GET

BAdI MRM_HEADER_CHECK

With this BAdI, you can execute additional checks on document header data, as well as item data.

- ▶ **Release**
  from SAP ECC 6.0
- ▶ **Call point**
  - ▶ Entry of incoming invoice
- ▶ **Method**
  - ▶ HEADERDATA_CHECK

BAdI MRM_HEADER_DEFAULT

With the method of this BAdI, you can copy default values to the header data of incoming invoices.

- ▶ **Release**
  from SAP R/3 4.7
- ▶ **Call points**
  - ▶ Transaction MIRO
  - ▶ Transaction MIRA
  - ▶ Transaction MIR7
- ▶ **Method**
  - ▶ HEADER_DEFAULT_SET

BAdI MRM_MRIS_HDAT_MODIFY

When you post a document with Transaction MRIS (invoicing plan settlement with Logistics Invoice Verification), you can change individual fields of the header data using this BAdI.

▶ **Release**
from SAP R/3 4.7

▶ **Call point**

  ▹ Transaction MRIS

▶ **Method**

  ▹ MRIS_HEADERDATA_MODIFY

BAdI MRM_MRIS_IDAT_MODIFY

When you post a document with Transaction MRIS (invoice plan settlement with Logistics Invoice Verification), you can change the document lines using this BAdI.

▶ **Release**
from SAP R/3 4.7

▶ **Call point**

  ▹ Transaction MRIS

▶ **Method**

  ▹ MRIS_ITEMDATA_MODIFY

BAdI MRM_MRKO_HDAT_MODIFY

In the consignment and pipeline settlement (RMVKON00 report), you can overwrite the supplier and the document type using this BAdI.

▶ **Release**
from SAP R/3 4.7

▶ **Call point**

  ▹ Report RMVKON00 (Transaction MRKO)

▶ **Method**

  ▹ MRKO_HEADERDATA_MODIFY

BAdI MRM_PAYMENT_TERMS

With this BAdI, you can check or change the terms of payment that have been copied from the purchase order or entered manually.

- **Release**
  from SAP R/3 4.7
- **Call point**
  - Entry of incoming invoice
- **Method**
  - PAYMENT_TERMS_SET

BAdI MRM_RELEASE_CHECK

During the release of locked incoming invoices in Transaction MRBR, you can use this BAdI to execute additional checks and prevent the release if applicable.

- **Release**
  from SAP R/3 4.7
- **Call point**
  - Transaction MRBR
- **Method**
  - DOCUMENT_CHECK_RELEASE

BAdI MRM_TOLERANCE_GROUP

You can usually assign only one tolerance group to one supplier. With this BAdI, you have the option to determine a tolerance group according to custom criteria during the invoice entry.

- **Release**
  from SAP R/3 4.7
- **Call point**
  - Entry of incoming invoice
- **Method**
  - TOLERANCE_GROUP_SET

BAdI MRM_TRANSACT_DEFAULT

When you enter incoming invoices, various fields are usually suggested depending on how the user filled them in previously. You can prepopulate these fields using this BAdI.

▶ **Release**
from SAP R/3 4.7

▶ **Call points**

  ▶ Transaction MIRO

  ▶ Transaction MIRA

  ▶ Transaction MIR7

▶ **Method**

  ▶ `TRANSACTION_DEFAULT_SET`

BAdI MRM_UDC_DISTRIBUTE

With this BAdI, you can change the distribution of unplanned delivery costs in the invoice items.

▶ **Release**
from SAP R/3 4.7

▶ **Call point**

  ▶ Entry of incoming invoice

▶ **Method**

  ▶ `AMOUNTS_CALCULATE`

BAdI MRM_WT_SPLIT_UPDATE

When you enter incoming invoices, you can use this BAdI to change the data on the withholding tax surcharge or on the amount split.

▶ **Release**
from SAP R/3 4.7

▶ **Call points**

  ▶ Transaction MIRO

  ▶ Transaction MIRA

  ▶ Transaction MIR7

- **Method**

  - WHTAX_SPLIT_UPDATE

BAdI MRM_VARIANCE_TYPE

Using this BAdI, you can fill the variance types in document items with custom values.

- **Release**
  from SAP ECC 6.0

- **Call points**

  - Transaction MIRO

  - Transaction MIR7

  - Transaction MIR6

- **Method**

  - DETERMINE

BAdI WRF_MRM_ASSIGN_TEST

You can customize the flow of the assignment test using the two methods of this BAdI.

- **Release**
  from SAP ECC 6.0

- **Call point**

  - Entry of incoming invoice

- **Methods**

  - DATES_REDETERMINE

  - INVOICE_SAVE

BAdI WRF_PREPAY_INVOICE

With the methods of this BAdI, you can change the posting date of a prepayment document or override the field PREPAYMENT RELEVANCE.

- **Release**
  following SAP ECC 6.0

- ▶ **Call point**
  - ▶ Entry of incoming invoice
- ▶ **Methods**
  - ▶ SET_POSTING_DATE
  - ▶ PREPAYMENT_RELEVANCE_CHANGE

BAdI MRM_INVOICE_UPDATE
(ES_BADI_INVOICE_UPDATE Enhancement Spot)

The methods of this BAdI run when the invoice documents are saved or deleted. You can define further checks or schedule follow-on processing here.

- ▶ **Release**
  from SAP ECC 6.0
- ▶ **Call points**
  - ▶ Transaction MIRO
  - ▶ Transaction MIR7
- ▶ **Methods**
  - ▶ PROCESS_AT_DELETE
  - ▶ PROCESS_AT_SAVE

BAdI MRM_PARTNER_CHECK
(ES_BADI_MRM_PARTNER Enhancement Spot)

Using this BAdI, you can check the invoice items to determine whether the business partner owns the suitable partner role to receive payments.

- ▶ **Release**
  from SAP ECC 6.0 (Enhancement Package 4, LOG_MMFI_P2P Business Function)
- ▶ **Call points**
  - ▶ Transaction MIRO
  - ▶ Transaction MIR7
  - ▶ Transaction MRBP (Report RMBABG00)
  - ▶ Transaction MRIS
  - ▶ Transaction MRRL
  - ▶ Transaction MRNB

- **Method**

  - CHECK_IP

BAdI MRM_DOWNPAYMENT
(ES_BADI_MRM_DOWNPAYMENT Enhancement Spot)

The message M8 318 ("Down payments for the Purchase Order ... available") is displayed upon entry of an invoice when such a down payment exists. With this BAdI, you can implement custom logic to check down payments and to prevent the message display if required.

- **Release**
  from SAP ECC 6.0 (Enhancement Package 4, LOG_MMFI_P2P Business Function)

- **Call points**

  - Transaction MIRO

  - Transaction MIR7

  - Transaction MIR4

  - Transaction MIR6

- **Method**

  - DOWNPAYMENT_CHECK

BAdI MRM_RETENTIONS
(ES_BADI_MRM_RETENTION Enhancement Spot)

Retention amounts are part of a new function that is being activated following Enhancement Package 4. With this, you can specify an amount that is retained at first, and will be paid only at the end of a specific period (e.g., by the end of a test phase). With this BAdI, you can automatically define the retention amount and partly override the field status of the input fields.

- **Release**
  from SAP ECC 6.0 (Enhancement Package 4, LOG_MMFI_P2P Business Function)

- **Call points**

  - Transaction MIRO

  - Transaction MIR7

  - Transaction MRBP (Report RMBABG00)

  - Transaction MRIS

▸ Transaction MRRL

▸ Transaction MRNB

▸ **Methods**

   ▸ CHANGE_PROPOSAL

   ▸ SET_PARAMETER

BAdI MRM_BLOCKREASON_DELETE_CUST (MRM_BLOCKREASON_DELETE Enhancement Spot)

When invoices are released (Transaction MRBR), you can use this BAdI to determine existing lock reasons and reset these if applicable.

▸ **Release**
from SAP ECC 6.0 (Enhancement Package 2, JFMIP_MM_01 Business Function)

▸ **Call point**

   ▸ Transaction MRBR

▸ **Methods**

   ▸ BLOCKREASON_POREF_CHECK

   ▸ BLOCKREASON_GLREF_CHECK

   ▸ BLOCKREASON_MATERIALREF_CHECK

MM08R002 Enhancement

You can use the following user exits in Logistics Invoice Verification to replace the tolerance checks when entering an invoice or to replace locked invoice to be released with a custom logic. You can find an example of this in Section 7.2, Overriding Tolerance Checks, in Chapter 7.

▸ **Release**
from SAP R/3 4.6C (or earlier)

▸ **Call points**

   ▸ Transaction MIRO

   ▸ Transaction MRBR

▸ **Components**

   ▸ EXIT_SAPLMR1M_001

- ▶ EXIT_SAPLMRMP_001

- ▶ EXIT_SAPLMRMC_001

LMR1M001 Enhancement

With the components of this enhancement, you can generate a default account assignment for blanket purchase orders, and check header and item data of invoices.

- ▶ **Release**
  from SAP R/3 4.6C (or earlier)

- ▶ **Call point**
  - ▶ Transaction MIRO

- ▶ **Components**
  - ▶ EXIT_SAPLMR1M_002
  - ▶ EXIT_SAPLMR1M_003 (obsolete after Release SAP R/3 4.6A)
  - ▶ EXIT_SAPLMRMP_010

LMR1M003 Enhancement

In this user exit, the header data and document items are provided to determine and return to a specific number range.

- ▶ **Release**
  from SAP R/3 4.6C (or earlier)

- ▶ **Call points**
  - ▶ Transaction MIRO
  - ▶ Transaction MIR7
  - ▶ Transaction MIRA

- ▶ **Component**
  - ▶ EXIT_SAPLMRME_003

LMR1M004 Enhancement

In this enhancement, various pieces of information at the header and item level of the document are provided to fill the item text (SGTXT field) when document items are entered. The item text is copied to the field of the accounting document of the same name.

▸ **Release**
from SAP R/3 4.6C (or earlier)

▸ **Call points**

- ▸ Transaction MIRO

- ▸ Transaction MIR7

- ▸ Transaction MIRA

▸ **Component**

- ▸ EXIT_SAPLMRMP_004

LMR1M005 Enhancement

When you post parked documents, you can indicate the document release relevant in this user exit. The document is then released via a workflow that you must design and implement yourself.

▸ **Release**
from SAP R/3 4.6C (or earlier)

▸ **Call points**

- ▸ Transaction MIR7

- ▸ Transaction MIR4

▸ **Component**

- ▸ EXIT_SAPLMRMC_002

LMR1M006 Enhancement

When posting XML invoices, you can revise the XML data before the actual BAPI_INCOMINGINVOICE_CREATE function module is called for the posting of the invoice.

▸ **Release**
from SAP R/3 4.6C (or earlier)

▸ **Call point**

- ▸ MRM_XMLBAPI_INCINV_CREATE

▸ **Component**

- ▸ EXIT_SAPLMRM_BAPI_001

RMVKON00 Enhancement

The user exits of this enhancement are called when the consignment stock and pipeline processing are called. You can influence the content of the invoice document prior to its update. Moreover, you can fill custom fields of the RWKA database table (consignment issues), which have been defined in the CI_RWKA append.

- ▶ **Release**
  from SAP R/3 4.6C (or earlier)
- ▶ **Call point**
  - ▶ Transaction MRKO (RMVKON00 report)
- ▶ **Components**
  - ▶ EXIT_RMVKON00_001
  - ▶ EXIT_RMVKON00_002

MRMH0001 Enhancement

This enhancement helps you to fill in or to change various fields from the document header and document item in the ERS procedure (Evaluated Receipt Settlement).

- ▶ **Release**
  from SAP R/3 4.6C (or earlier)
- ▶ **Call point**
  - ▶ Transaction MRRL
- ▶ **Components**
  - ▶ EXIT_SAPLMRMH_001
  - ▶ EXIT_SAPLMRMH_002

MRMH0002 Enhancement

If the invoice receipt is generated in the EDI procedure, you can use the user exits of this enhancement to determine and define some additional data. Among this data are the company code, supplier, tax code, and the assignment to a purchase order item or a delivery note number. In the EXIT_SAPLMRMH_014 module, and in the EXIT_SAPLMRMH_015 module of the formatted invoice document shortly prior to the actual updating, you are also provided with the complete IDoc segment.

- ▶ **Release**
  from SAP R/3 4.6C (or earlier)

- ▶ **Call point**
  - ▶ IDOC_INPUT_INVOIC_MRM

- ▶ **Components**
  - ▶ EXIT_SAPLMRMH_011
  - ▶ EXIT_SAPLMRMH_012
  - ▶ EXIT_SAPLMRMH_013
  - ▶ EXIT_SAPLMRMH_014
  - ▶ EXIT_SAPLMRMH_015

MRMH0003 Enhancement

When you reevaluate an invoice document via the RMMR1MRB report using these two user exits, you have access to the header data and the item data of the invoice.

- ▶ **Release**
  from SAP R/3 4.6C (or earlier)
- ▶ **Call point**
  - ▶ Transaction MRNB (Report RMMR1MRB)
- ▶ **Components**
  - ▶ EXIT_RMMR1MRB_001
  - ▶ EXIT_RMMR1MRB_002

MRMN0001 Enhancement

Various user exits are provided when outbound messages of the invoice check are processed. In the case of the EDI shipping, you can change the IDoc data and the IDoc control record, and you can control which data is to be displayed via different icons in the print output. Furthermore, you can influence whether the invoice document is to be created depending on the messages found.

- ▶ **Release**
  from SAP R/3 4.6C (or earlier)
- ▶ **Call point**
  - ▶ Transaction MIRO
- ▶ **Components**
  - ▶ EXIT_SAPLMRMN_001

▶ EXIT_SAPLMRMN_002

▶ EXIT_SAPLMRMN_003

A.5.2 Archiving

The enhancements for the archiving implemented in this section have been added with Enhancement Package 4 to SAP ECC 6.0.

BAdI ARC_MM_REBEL_CHECK

This BAdI is used to execute custom checks for the archivability in the write program of invoice documents.

▶ **Release**
from SAP ECC 6.0 (Enhancement Package 4)

▶ **Call point**

   ▶ Write Program RM08RW47

▶ **Method**

   ▶ CHECK

BAdI ARC_MM_REBEL_WRITE

With this BAdI, you can enhance the volume of archiving of the write program for invoice documents with other database tables, for example, custom tables with custom data.

▶ **Release**
from SAP ECC 6.0 (Enhancement Package 4)

▶ **Call point**

   ▶ Write Program RM08RW47

▶ **Method**

   ▶ WRITE

A.5.3 Conventional Invoice Verification

The following user exits are run only in conventional Invoice Verification, which has been replaced by Logistics Invoice Verification and can no longer be used after Release 4.7.

MM08R001 Enhancement

This enhancement helps you to fill or to change various fields from the document header and document item in the ERS procedure (Evaluated Receipt Settlement).

▶ **Release**
   from SAP R/3 4.6C (or earlier)

▶ **Call point**
   ▸ Transaction MR01

▶ **Components**
   ▸ EXIT_RMMR01RS_001
   ▸ EXIT_RMMR01RS_002
   ▸ EXIT_RMMR01RS_003
   ▸ EXIT_RMMR01RS_004

MM08R002 Enhancement

You can use the following user exits in the conventional Invoice Verification to replace the tolerance checks when an invoice is entered, or to replace a locked invoice to be released with a custom logic.

▶ **Release**
   from SAP R/3 4.6C (or earlier)

▶ **Call points**
   ▸ Transaction MR01
   ▸ Transaction MR02

▶ **Components**
   ▸ EXIT_SAPMM08A_001
   ▸ EXIT_SAPMM08R_001
   ▸ EXIT_SAPLKONT_002

B   The Author

 **Jürgen Schwaninger** is a freelance SAP consultant, and following his original training as an industrial administrator in 1993, went on to graduate as a business information technologist. Since 1999, he has been working as a consultant in the area of SAP logistics and ABAP programming, and also regularly holds training sessions as a lecturer for ABAP and Web Dynpro ABAP.

Jürgen has been working in SAP Remote Consulting since 2001 and has dealt with complex customer queries in the areas of Materials Management (MM) and Sales and Distribution (SD), as well as in other aspects of logistics. This work includes devising solutions for customer-specific problems through recommendations in the standard and adaptations in Customizing, developing user exits and BAdIs, modifying standard or process recommendations, and developing customer-specific programs.

He has also been involved in numerous projects in Germany and abroad, including one of the first projects for the implementation of SAP R/3 4.7 at a major Swedish packaging manufacturer.

Jürgen Schwaninger lives with his wife and two children in Bruchsal in the German federal state of Baden-Württemberg.

Index